WE COME TO LIFE with THOSE WE SERVE

WE COME TO LIFE WITH THOSE WE SERVE

RICHARD B. GUNDERMAN

INDIANA UNIVERSITY PRESS

This book is a publication of

Indiana University Press
Office of Scholarly Publishing
Herman B Wells Library 350
1320 East 10th Street
Bloomington, Indiana 47405 USA

iupress.indiana.edu

♾ The paper used in this publication meets the minimum
requirements of the American National Standard for Information
Sciences—Permanence of Paper for Printed Library Materials,
ANSI Z39.48–1992.

Manufactured in the United States of America

Cataloging information is available from the Library of Congress.

ISBN 978-0-253-02967-6 (cloth)
ISBN 978-0-253-03101-3 (paperback)
ISBN 978-0-253-03102-0 (ebook)

1 2 3 4 5   22 21 20 19 18 17

CONTENTS

Acknowledgments   vii

Introduction: Old Stories and New Life   1

one   Victor: The Life Devoid of Service   5

two   Ivan: Death through Self-Absorption   14

three   Albert: Service to the Suffering   25

four   Rebecca: Service to Family   36

five   Benjamin: Service to Community   45

six   Alexander: Service through Suffering   56

seven   John: Service through Education   65

eight   Bill: Service through Commerce   75

nine   Ebenezer: The Spirit of Service   84

ten   Vincent: Service through Art   97

Afterword: The Life of Service   103

ACKNOWLEDGMENTS

SHARING BROUGHT THIS BOOK TO LIFE. MY PARENTS, JAMES AND MARILYN, shared curiosity and wonder. Bill Van Voorhies shared a belief that his charges could write. Eric Dean and Bill Placher shared the life of the mind. Jim Gustafson, David Grene, Leon Kass, Leszek Kolakowski, Mark Siegler, Norma Wagoner, and Karl Weintraub shared what it means to take ideas seriously. Mervyn Cohen shared a home. Bob Payton and Paul Nagy shared the virtues of good conversation, a way of life that continues with Matt Boulton, Bill Enright, Tom Gunderman, Bill McGraw, and especially Mark Mutz. Students too numerous to name have shared more insights than I can count. And most of all I have been blessed to share life with Laura and the four people with whom we have tried hardest to share the most, Rebecca, Peter, David, and John.

WE COME TO LIFE with THOSE WE SERVE

INTRODUCTION

Old Stories and New Life

NEW STORIES CAN HAVE A PROBLEM—THEY CAN PREVENT US FROM encountering the old ones. The same can be said for the news. Focusing on recent news distracts us from old news. Just because something is new—whether in fashion, politics, business, sports, literature, philosophy, or theology—does not mean that it is improved.

Over a vast expanse of time, nations have been founded, wars fought, discoveries made, systems of belief developed, and geniuses have come and gone. Viewing the latest news in corporate mergers or consumer electronics with this in mind, it seems improbable that the events of today, or this week, or even this year are as momentous as we might suppose. To find our place in the world and make the most of our lives, we need to operate with a longer sense of time.

Here, in part, lies the purpose of this book. Our lives can be only as good as the books we read, the conversations we have, and the habits of mind we carry with us through every day.

It has been said that we are what we eat. The same might be said for what we read, because what we read can powerfully shape what we talk about and the stories we tell ourselves. Too often, a sober examination of these stories reveals bad news—it is possible to be glutted with information yet starving for real insight. The information age has left many of us overfed but undernourished, longing for some way of making sense of the world that enables us to distinguish between the incidental and the genuinely significant.

In his book *The Mind of a Mnemonist: A Little Book about a Vast Memory*, the Russian neurologist A. R. Luria describes the extraordinary case of Solomon Shereshevsky, a man who seemed to remember everything. Apparently without effort and after only a single hearing, he could recall speeches word for word, memorize complex mathematical formulas, and even recite poetry in languages he did not understand. This might seem like a great gift—to recall what happens in each moment such that it never slips away. However, the mnemonist's intelligence was only average, and he experienced great difficulty forgetting. He struggled to distinguish the merely incidental from the genuinely significant.

This is the challenge—telling the difference between what is worth remembering, knowing, and etching into our hearts and what is of no more than passing interest. There is nothing inherently pernicious about the latest stock quotations, box scores, or celebrity chinwag. It is, after all, information. Yet continuous immersion in information powerfully shapes our habits of mind and heart. We tend to become what we habitually attend to, and if we develop the habit of attending to drivel, then our lives will tend to matter less because they are so poorly attuned to what really matters.

The metaphor of tuning is a revealing one. Each person is like a radio receiver, which gravitates toward certain frequencies. Extensive sections of bandwidth are devoted to silliness, ideas that will be forgotten almost as soon as they are heard or uttered. But somewhere on the dial are different conversations that hold out the possibility of more enduring enlightenment. To stand a chance of tuning to these frequencies, we must first wrench ourselves away from the static.

Think of a library. Suppose two people enter a huge library. One person proceeds to the periodical section, spending the day perusing magazines that fan the flames of consumer passion, replete with glossy images of extravagant cars, jewelry, houses, cosmetics, electronics, and beverages. The implicit message of these magazines seems to be this—to find satisfaction in life, we need to buy things, and the better the things we buy, the more satisfied we are likely to be. Our mission, then, is to get lots of money so that we can buy lots of nice things.

Yet as William Wordsworth reminds us, "Getting and spending, we lay waste our powers."

The other person repairs to a very different section of the library—perhaps religion, philosophy, or literature. There, the message of the sacred texts, philosophical inquiries, and great novels and poetry is quite different. Instead of getting and spending, human life is shaped above all by what we know, what we believe in, and what we care about. If we know what we most need to know, believe what we most need to believe, and care about what most deserves our dedication, we stand a chance of leading lives that really count for something. It is not what we have but who we are striving to become that brings us to life.

It offends our egalitarian, live-and-let-live, to-each-his-or-her-own sensibilities to say so, but how we spend our time matters. Each year, day, and minute we waste on drivel escalates the probability that the next year, day, or minute will be much the same. By contrast, the more deeply we engrain the habit of attending to what is real, the more likely we are to make something worthy of our lives. We are not simply mouthing a preexisting script. Instead we actively script our lives every day.

To exist is good, but it is not enough. Survival beats the alternative, but not at any cost. The aim is not simply to exist or survive but to live as fully as possible, and this means devoting our lives to purposes that transcend ourselves.

Wealth, power, and fame are dangerous not because they are inherently corrupt, but because they instill in us the habit of letting lower things supersede higher ones. As long as the lower things are on top, we lead lives that can only be described as upside down.

This book's ten chapters are opportunities to reexamine our lives and determine which end is really up. Populated in part by other books, it engages others' stories in hopes that they can unlock a deeper understanding of our own. Where a book is not the touchstone, an individual who led an illuminating life is the focus. Each chapter can serve as a mirror, inviting us to ask what purposes our lives are devoted to and challenging us to survey the gap that separates the person we are from the person we aspire to become. The distinction in play is between not right and wrong but the shallow and the deep.

We need to find life paths of genuine substance that we can lay down and follow for the sake of something beautiful, good, and true. No matter how much worldly success we may achieve, leading a superficial life is simply too high a price to pay for the privilege. It means selling our birthright—the richness of a life fully lived—for a mess of pottage. Like anything truly worthy, following a path of substance requires clarity of vision and sustained effort. Yet the effort we invest in real reading, real self-examination, and real conversation makes real life possible.

Many of us are called to rediscover the joy of good reading and conversation. The most fitting books come from a variety of historical periods, forms of discourse, and points of view. In the chapters that follow, I aim to demonstrate, in broad outline, an approach to reading and conversing that can bring such books and stories—and those who read them—to life. A book's pages may be as dry as dust, but few things are as enlivening as great stories.

These stories derive from both fiction and nonfiction, treating both literary characters and historical figures as equally illuminating. A great work of the imagination—at least in the spirit at work here—can prove every bit as edifying as a historical account. In fact, a person could devote large swathes of life to reading nothing but newspapers yet never approach the depth of insight afforded by the best novels, poems, and works of art. What merely happened and the forces at work in the hearts of human beings are two different things, and the latter is a subject on which both biographical and literary approaches have much to offer.

In some cases, the stories presented and discussed here can best be understood as cautionary tales, portrayals of how seriously life can go wrong when we are distracted, disoriented, or frankly subverted. Often the best way to appreciate the full magnitude of the stakes in life is to spend some time with lives gone wrong. The purpose is not to condemn the lost but to recognize that every one of us can, in many different ways, go astray, losing sight of both the journey and the stars by which we steer.

Other stories are of a more exemplary nature, directly evocative of goodness. Such stories can remedy one of our most deadly contemporary afflictions: inspiration deficit disorder.

To work well, we must learn to live well. To live well, we must learn to read well. And to read well, many of us must learn to read anew. Through stories, we can learn to share better, and by sharing better we can bring each other to life.

The thesis—or perhaps riddle—at the heart of this book is this: We come to life not through grasping, hoarding, or ostentatious display, but by recognizing and seizing opportunities to serve.

one

VICTOR
The Life Devoid of Service

LIFE IS A GIFT. NONE OF US CREATED OURSELVES OUT OF NOTHING, AND each of us is here thanks in part to circumstances far beyond our control. When sperm and egg join and a new life is created, we are not around to direct or even spectate as events unfold. So, too, development in utero takes place without our awareness. Each of us is there for birth, yet none orchestrates or even understands what is happening. Even as infants, we are helpless and utterly dependent on the care of others for food, warmth, shelter, and everything else we need to survive.

As children and adolescents, this dependence gradually diminishes somewhat over time. Yet even today, as adults, how many of us can honestly claim to be self-sufficient? Though capable of contributing to our own sustenance, we remain remarkably dependent—perhaps interdependent—on others for the food we eat, the clothes we wear, the dwellings we inhabit, and virtually every other material good on which our lives depend.

Working in a hospital, I am regularly reminded of how quickly the gift of life can be lost. Just a few weeks ago, a number of injured children were transported to our hospital's emergency department. A father had been driving children to school one morning when their vehicle was struck by another. Two of the children died within hours, and a third died in the following days. Another child will live each day of his life bearing scars of the incident, including permanent disabilities.

Such devastating incidents call to mind the fragility of existence—the fact that, in an instant, our lives can lurch in a radically different direction, or even be wrenched entirely away from us. We can take steps to protect ourselves and those we love, but even something as basic as the continuation of life is never completely in our own hands. Just a tiny alteration in the electrical rhythms of our hearts and—poof!—in the short space of a few minutes any of us can be wiped permanently from this earthly stage.

Life is something given, not something we invent, make, or own. We do not begin in a state of nonexistence or limbo and then fight our way to life. Instead, we become self-aware and live out every moment of our lives in a state of given-ness.

The principal problem with calling life a gift is a profound asymmetry between receiver and giver. We know exactly and in great detail to whom the gift has been given—to each of us. Whether we are talking about our own lives or those of our spouses, children, and friends, we know well what has been received. Less clear, however, is the source of these gifts, the benefactor.

This can make it difficult to know to whom or to what our gratitude—or in the case of deeply afflicted individuals such as Job, our outrage—should be directed. Except perhaps in the pages of sacred scriptures, the gift of life comes with no card revealing the identity and intentions of the one who gives. To some for whom the giver is unknown, it is very difficult to think of life as a gift. Even in this case, however, many are ready to admit life's given-ness.

There are countless ways by which the arc between life's giver and receiver might have been interrupted. At the very beginning, any of a number of contraceptive techniques might have been used to prevent fertilization or implantation of an egg. A pregnancy might have come to an end, either accidentally or by intention. Parents might have abandoned or even abused their offspring, or simply have parented so carelessly that life ended in infancy or childhood. With increasing age, life can be ended by its possessor, through so simple a mistake as crossing a street without looking or operating a vehicle carelessly. In some cases, people choose to take their own lives.

Science and technology have presented us with another perspective from which to view the gift of life—namely, that of the giver. One familiar example is the care we are now capable of providing infants who are born prematurely. Fifty years ago, an infant born at twenty-six or twenty-eight weeks of gestation had virtually no chance of survival. Even President John Kennedy and his wife, Jackie— parents with every advantage of wealth and power—lost such a child, their son Patrick, who was born in 1963 five and a half weeks prematurely.

Today, by contrast, new medications and support techniques have made it possible to save the lives of many such infants, allowing these tiny human beings to grow up and lead normal lives. One crucial step on this road has been the discovery and manufacture of pulmonary surfactant, a substance normally present in the lungs that dramatically decreases the amount of work required to expand them. When it is missing, infants exhaust themselves simply trying to breathe. Thanks to such new drugs, contemporary medicine is able to give many premature infants their lives back.

But the ambitions do not stop with sustaining lives that would otherwise end. Some people have called for biomedical science and technology to carry the fight farther, extending the human lifespan and perhaps even conquering mortality itself. To some—especially those most convinced of their own importance— the fact that we die represents an outrage that can undermine all enjoyment of life. Some wealthy individuals are investing heavily in just this conquest. They hope that advances in genetics, proteomics, and other biological sciences will soon make it possible to keep human beings alive far longer than ever thought possible.

Others, perhaps convinced that the biological basis of aging and death is too deeply woven into our fiber, are calling on artificial intelligence to do the same job, by making it possible to transfer a person's memory into computer circuitry. Whether or not this would represent life in any recognizable sense is open for debate, but the fundamental ambition—to take the reins of life and death into our own hands—holds immense appeal.

The urge to take ownership of life, transforming it from a gift that we receive but cannot earn into an achievement that we control, is powerful, and also venerable. It found no greater expression than in one of the very first science fiction novels ever written—Mary Shelley's *Frankenstein*. Nowhere else has an author thought through more deeply the implications of humans becoming creators in our own right. By exploring Shelley's portrait of the ambition to seize life's reins, we can see more clearly what it means to understand life as a gift.

Shelley's monster—who unexpectedly turns out to be less the creature than the creature's creator, Victor Frankenstein—represents the antithesis of someone who experiences life as a gift. In the original sense, a monster is a portent or warning. Abnormal or especially large creatures were often regarded as signs or omens of impending disaster. Perhaps the failure to understand life as a gift—to attempt to make life purely a matter of our own will—represents one such disaster.

Mary Shelley

Before turning to the novel, it is helpful to know something of its author's life, which in many respects is no less extraordinary. Mary Shelley was born of two famously brilliant parents. Her father, William Godwin (1756–1836), was a British journalist, political philosopher, and novelist whose name is linked with the founding of utilitarianism, a school of ethical and political thought which defines as most desirable that course of action which produces the best consequences for the most people. In addition, he was an important proponent of anarchy, the view that human beings are governed best when they govern themselves through voluntary institutions. His book *Things as They Are; or, The Adventures of Caleb Williams* (1794), is often regarded as the first mystery novel.

Among Godwin's regular conversation partners were many extraordinary individuals: the poet Samuel Taylor Coleridge, the writer Charles Lamb, the American politician Aaron Burr, and the poet Percy Bysshe Shelley. Godwin believed in the perfectibility of human beings and human society, arguing that if the corrupting influences of society could be sufficiently reduced, evil could be expunged from human nature. He once wrote, "Perfectibility is one of the most unequivocal characteristics of the human species," perhaps helping to set the stage for his daughter's first novel.

Shelley's mother was her father's undoubted intellectual peer. Mary Wollstonecraft (1759–1797) was an English writer and philosopher who ranks as one of history's most important advocates of women's rights. Her work *A Vindication of the Rights of Women* (1792) argues that women are naturally the equals of men and that the only reason they may appear less intelligent is the fact that they are deprived of an equal education. To realize a vision of equality, the reason of women must be as fully developed as the reason of men: "It would be an endless task to trace the variety of meanness, cares, and sorrows, into which women are plunged by the prevailing opinion that they were created rather to feel than to reason, and that all the power they obtain, must be obtained by their charms and weakness."

Like her husband, Wollstonecraft believed that human beings naturally seek the good: "No man chooses evil because it is evil; he only mistakes it for happiness, the good he seeks." If only people could see things aright, she believed, they would naturally choose what is best.

Yet for many years, Wollstonecraft's personal life gained more attention than her writings. It generally focused on two ill-fated love affairs, one of which led to the birth of her first daughter. She married Godwin in 1797, the same year she gave birth to her second daughter, Mary. She contracted childbed fever and died eleven days later at the age of thirty-eight.

The third crucial player in the drama of Mary Shelley's early life is Percy Bysshe Shelley (1792–1822), whom she married as a teenager. Born the illegitimate son of a member of Parliament, Shelley eventually matriculated at University College, Oxford, where be published a pamphlet entitled "The Necessity of Atheism," which got him expelled from the university in 1811. His father negotiated to get him reinstated on condition that Shelley recant his views, but he refused to do so. Against his father's wishes, the nineteen-year-old Shelley eloped with a sixteen-year-old boarding school student, Harriet Westbrook.

When he later met Mary through her father William Godwin, he fell madly in love with her, threatening suicide if she did not love him in return. Though he was largely unknown in his own day, today Shelley is considered one of the greatest of the Romantic poets, particularly for such works as *Ozymandias* and *Prometheus Unbound*. In what follows, both will prove significant. An excerpt from the former reads:

> I met a traveller from an antique land
> Who said: "Two vast and trunkless legs of stone
> Stand in the desert . . . Near them, on the sand,
> Half sunk, a shattered visage lies, whose frown,
> And wrinkled lip, and sneer of cold command,
> Tell that its sculptor well those passions read
> Which yet survive, stamped on these lifeless things,
> The hand that mocked them, and the heart that fed:
> And on the pedestal these words appear:
> 'My name is Ozymandias, king of kings:
> Look on my works, ye Mighty, and despair!'"

Shelley also seems to have played an important role in shaping the economic thinking of Karl Marx, as well as the high regard for nonviolent resistance of Leo Tolstoy and Mohandas Gandhi. He died at the age of twenty-nine in what is now Italy in a boating accident.

Mary Wollstonecraft Shelley (1797–1851) grew up without her mother and burdened by a sense of responsibility for her mother's death. Mary and her older half-sister, Fanny, were raised by their father, who provided them a first-rate education. When Mary was just sixteen years old, she and Percy Shelley fell in love, soon eloping to the European Continent, along with Mary's stepsister. There they were ostracized and faced severe debts. They also suffered the loss of a daughter who was born prematurely.

While in Europe they spent a summer at Lake Geneva, Switzerland, with the notorious poet Lord Byron and his physician, John Polidori. There Byron proposed a contest to see who could write the best ghost story. Polidori rose to the occasion by crafting the first vampire story. Mary Shelley, who initially faced writer's block, eventually responded with the outlines of *Frankenstein*. Writing years later, she described a "waking dream" in which "I saw the pale student of the unhallowed arts kneeling beside the thing he had put together. I saw the hideous phantasm of a man stretched out, and then, on the working of some powerful engine, show signs of life, and stir with an uneasy, half-vital motion. Frightful must it be, for supremely frightful would be the effect of any human endeavor to mock the stupendous mechanism of the Creator of the world." She subsequently developed the story into a novel and published it two years later in 1818, when she was twenty-one years old. Percy died just four years later. Mary raised their only surviving child, Percy Florence Shelley, and continued to write short stories, plays, essays, and biographies, dying of a brain tumor at the age of fifty-three.

Victor Frankenstein

Published anonymously, the full title of her book is *Frankenstein; or, the Modern Prometheus*. Prometheus, whose name means "forethought," is the mythological ancient Greek Titan who steals fire from Zeus and gives it to proto-human creatures dwelling in the darkness of caves, thereby bringing them light and warmth, effectively conferring humanity on them. As punishment for his disobedience, Zeus has Prometheus chained to a rock, where his liver (understood to be the source of life, hence its name) is eaten every day by an eagle.

Frankenstein is an epistolary novel, written as a series of letters from a fictional character named Robert Walton to his sister. A failed writer, Walton has decided to embark on an ocean voyage to the North Pole in hopes of achieving fame by advancing scientific knowledge. During the voyage, he and his crew see a gigantic figure traveling across the ice by dogsled. Hours later, a nearly frozen and starved man who identifies himself as Victor Frankenstein appears and states that he is in pursuit of the giant. Seeing in Walton the same overarching ambition that once animated him, the convalescent Frankenstein proceeds to recount the sad, cautionary tale of his life.

Frankenstein is born to a wealthy Geneva family that encourages him to develop his passion for science. As he prepares to leave for university, his mother dies of an infectious disease, only increasing his scientific ardor. He soon begins devoting all his time and energy to developing a technique that can restore life to inanimate matter. This eventually leads him to create the creature, often in later years referred to as "Frankenstein," though never so in Shelley's novel. In an effort to surpass nature, Frankenstein makes the creature larger than life, eight feet tall. But his expectations of perfection are quickly dashed: "His limbs were in proportion, and I had selected his features as beautiful. Beautiful! Great God! His yellow skin scarcely covered the work of muscles and arteries beneath; his hair was of a lustrous black, and flowing; his teeth of a pearly whiteness; but these luxuriances only formed a more horrid contrast with his watery eyes, which seemed almost of the same color as the dun-white sockets in which they were set, his shriveled complexion and straight black lips."

The creature he intended to be perfect, a sort of superman, proves instead to be hideous, and as soon as he sees it stir, Frankenstein flees in horror. The monster eventually teaches itself to speak and read, but all its attempts to establish human contact are thwarted by its frightening appearance. It begs Frankenstein to relieve its loneliness by creating a female companion, but the creator cannot bear the thought that such creatures might begin to propagate, and so refuses. In vengeance, the creature kills the people dearest to its maker, including Frankenstein's young brother, his best friend, and, on the night of their marriage, his new wife.

Though Frankenstein gives life to the creature, he never assumes parental responsibility for it. He refuses to raise and educate it. He never even gives it a name. Throughout the book, the creature is simply referred to as "the monster," "the fiend," "the demon," and "it." Frankenstein seems to think that the giving of life is a purely technical problem and that, disappointed by the result, he is free to abandon his creation.

The creature, on the other hand, desperately longs for a parent, someone to love and care for it. It tells Frankenstein, "Remember that I am thy creature: I ought to be thy Adam, but I am rather thy fallen angel, whom thou drivest from joy for no misdeed." What has the creature ever done to merit revulsion and abandonment? Initially nothing—like any newborn baby, the creature enters the world innocent of wrongdoing. Yet Frankenstein abhors it nonetheless, and eventually that which he spurns lashes out at him, destroying what he loves.

The Monster

Victor Frankenstein, the "modern Prometheus," is engaged in an extraordinarily prideful activity, effectively assuming a divine role. Imagining what his efforts will mean once he has succeeded, he muses: "A new species would bless me as its creator and source; many happy and excellent natures would owe their being to me.

No father could claim the gratitude of his child so completely as I should deserve theirs." Literally, Frankenstein is playing God. He envisions a new species that would "bless" him as creator. These creatures would be happy and excellent and would owe their being to him, a debt that they would presumably continuously strive long and hard to repay.

Frankenstein would be honored and venerated as no human being has ever been venerated—not merely as a liberator or savior but as a creator, the very source of life. The gratitude owed to him would be unprecedented, in part because he would be more than a father. Having for the first time created life without the collaboration of a mother, the devotion normally due two parents would flow entirely to him. Yet, as we have seen, Frankenstein finds within himself not even a hint of parental sentiment.

Frankenstein is guilty of a kind of monomania of the sort hinted at by the founders of the modern scientific method, men such as Francis Bacon and René Descartes. He describes such natural philosophers, whom we would today call scientists, as having acquired "new and almost unlimited powers; they can command the thunders of heaven, mimic the earthquake, and even mock the invisible world with its own shadows." Before long, the natural sciences, and in particular the new science of chemistry, become nearly his sole occupation.

Although the scientific method reveals much, it does not reveal everything. Taken to an extreme, devotion to it may actually blind its practitioner to other realities. Frankenstein knows how to harvest tissues, knit them together, and stir them to life, but he does not understand the contents of the human heart. He is technically prophetic but humanly blind. If life means animating matter, he is a genius, but if it means nurturing the capacity to love, he is an idiot.

Frankenstein's project is also reductionistic in the extreme. He understands each of the parts but fails to grasp the whole. He thinks that if he collects all the best components of a human being, he need only stitch them together to produce a creature nothing less than perfect. But his perfect parts produce a monstrous whole, evoking not adoration but fear and loathing: "The dissecting room and the slaughterhouse furnished many of my materials, and often did my human nature turn with loathing from my occupation, whilst, still urged on by an eagerness which perpetually increased, I brought my work near to a conclusion." Far from deepening his humanity, playing the role of creator forces Frankenstein to deny it. Something inside him warns him that the work in which he is engaged is repugnant and inhuman, but he is pushed on by eagerness and ambition to set himself up as a god.

He is like the makers of the Tower of Babel in the Bible, who sought to build their way to heaven and supplant the gods. But the price he pays for his vaunting ambition is far greater than he could imagine. In treating life as a purely technical problem, he ends up not creating life, but destroying it. Everything he holds dear—his family, his experiments, and even his own life—is ruined. In short, Victor Frankenstein is egregiously irresponsible. His creature completed, "The beauty of the dream vanished, and breathless horror and disgust filled my heart. Unable to endure the aspect of the being I had created, I rushed out of the room." This lack of responsibility represents a devastating human failure, at the level not of moral principle, but of the heart. Frankenstein is brilliant, but he is devoid of love, and without love, nothing human can grow or flourish. Says his unloved creature, "Believe me, Frankenstein, I was benevolent; my soul glowed with love and humanity: but am I not alone, miserably alone? You, my creator, abhor me; what hope can I gather from your fellow-creatures, who owe me nothing? They spurn and hate me." Rejected by its own creator, the person from whom love should flow most naturally, the creature quite rightly perceives little hope of love from any human being. Its good nature has been twisted by repeated rejection, the inability to find even a conversation partner or companion, let alone someone to love and love in return. Though born "benevolent and good," misery has made the creature a "fiend."

Frankenstein is a novel about love, and in particular, the disastrous consequences of life devoid of it. In particular, the novel is completely lacking in maternal love, in part because it is nearly devoid of mothers. Again and again, mothers or potential mothers in the novel die or are killed off. It is the death of Frankenstein's mother that leads him to his unhallowed experiments. His wife is killed on their wedding night. And Frankenstein himself is utterly unfit to play the role of mother.

Author Mary Shelley herself knew what it was like to grow up motherless, bearing a heavy measure of guilt over her mother's death. Her efforts to become a mother herself were likewise repeatedly thwarted by the death of her infant and multiple miscarriages.

Victor Frankenstein, in some ways a great man, is also the novel's greatest monster, precisely because he does not love, and through his lack of love he produces a living, breathing monster. Frankenstein gives, but his purpose in giving is not focused on the recipient—the creature itself or the species to which he wishes to serve as benefactor. Instead the creator's efforts are all about the creator himself, Victor Frankenstein. In seeking to win godlike powers and adoration for himself, he is in fact thinking only of himself. When things do not go well, he asks only what it means for him. Convinced of his own unprecedented importance, he cannot see his life-giving project from any perspective but his own.

This would-be philanthropist and benefactor of humankind turns out, quite predictably, to be a monstrous misanthrope. Like William Godwin, perhaps, he believed in the ultimate perfectibility of human beings, but he did not grasp the inherent limitations of our nature. Like Mary Wollstonecraft, he thought no person chooses evil, failing to recognize what evil really means. And like Percy Shelley's *Ozymandias*, he thought others would look upon his works and despair, never suspecting that, because of his pride, the final despair would be his own.

Victor Frankenstein was brilliant but not wise. As a result, his victory (the meaning of his given name) contained the seeds of his inevitable defeat. He lost not because of a misfire, but precisely because he hit his target. Anticipating the culmination of his project, he had forecast that "what had been the study and desire of the wisest men since the creation of the world was now within my grasp."

But had the wisest men truly studied what Frankenstein studied? Had they devoted their lives to unlocking the mysteries of life and death, understood as the technical challenges of bringing the dead back to life? Had the conquest of death in fact been their central desire?

Or were they in fact pursuing something else? Perhaps the wisest human beings are defined not by their ability to co-opt divine prerogatives but by their recognition of the grave folly of seeking to do so. Perhaps true wisdom does not mean surmounting our humanity and making gods of ourselves, but rather striving to lead good human lives by becoming as fully human as we can.

What would full humanity look like? If *Frankenstein* is any guide, it consists not of rejecting our humanity, but of embracing it. It means facing up to our own mortality and seeking to make every day count. It means realizing as fully as possible the possibilities for love. It is not through persisting but through loving that we stand the best chance of really living.

If we come to life through those we serve, then Frankenstein did not lead much of a life. He served no one but himself and his own grand ambitions. His dreams of becoming humanity's greatest benefactor were ultimately about himself, with humanity as his cheering section. He was with no one, and as a result he served no one. And because he did not serve, he never really came to life. Almost from the first moment, he failed to breathe life into his creation and instead destroyed it, returning it to the death from which he had pirated it.

Shelley's story serves as a reminder that there is a difference between mere life and truly living. It is possible to exhibit all the signs of life recognized by biology—growth, development, reproduction, and so on—and all the vital signs that physicians assess—pulse, breathing, blood pressure, and temperature—and yet still be going through life half alive, barely aware of what is going on. Over the course of a life, some days pass in a blur, barely registering. On other days, a high level of engagement produces memories that last a lifetime.

The question is, what distinguishes the empty days from the full ones? Numerous factors play a role, such as whether or not a major historical event has occurred. Yet one of the most important turns out to be whether we have made a difference in the life of another person. Service adds zest to a day in a way that mere amusement and self-gratification cannot. When one life touches another, a spark is ignited, a spark that can generate real warmth and light.

two

IVAN

Death through Self-Absorption

SOME TRUTHS ARE MOMENTOUS AND UNIVERSAL. CONSIDER, FOR EXAMPLE, the ancient Confucian teaching, "He who seeks the good of others has already secured his own." This dictum does not arise from the experience of any particular person or find application in any specific situation. It applies across the board to all people at all times. As long as we think first of ourselves, others are unlikely to count on or care very much about us. On the other hand, if we seek first to make a difference for others, our lives stand a better chance of amounting to something.

Other truths are more subtle and seemingly idiosyncratic. Seeking to convey truth, some great minds have produced commandments and counsels, often couched in the imperative, such as the familiar "Thou shalt not." Others have chosen to tell stories, providing accounts of particular people in particular sets of circumstances. To these latter minds, truth is not an overarching moral imperative but a series of insights that emerge through the particularities of unfolding daily life, involving specific people, events, and relationships. To these thinkers, narratives are truer to life than moral codes.

One such writer is Leo Tolstoy, perhaps the greatest novelist who ever lived, whose novels and short stories are full of details that often seem, at first glance, to be purely incidental. How a character such as Karenin in *Anna Karenina* enters a room and what Natasha in *War and Peace* notices first upon meeting someone might seem purely arbitrary, but in Tolstoy's hands even the tiniest details offer deep insights into a person. We could ask such characters to write down their credos, but something far deeper and more authentic is illuminated by simply watching them in action.

To understand just how badly wrong a life can go, we often do better not by comparing that life to a set of moral injunctions—do not lie, do not steal, do not covet what others have—but by carefully studying that life. What, for example, does a life look like when lived purely for itself, and what price do people on such a path pay for making themselves the center of their own universe? One answer, implicit in the Confucian dictum but brought fully to life only in the context of a life story, is this: Such a person is quite likely to end up isolated and lonely.

One of the most harrowing portraits of isolation—the polar opposite of working, living, and being with others—is found in perhaps the greatest novella ever composed: Leo Tolstoy's *The Death of Ivan Ilych*. On the surface, Tolstoy's story appears to recount the life of a nineteenth-century Russian judge who contracts a terminal illness and then wrestles with the possibility that his life has been devoid of meaning.

In fact, however, the life of Ivan Ilych Golovin is far more troubling: It is a tale of the ordinary yet disturbing wages of a life devoted purely to self. Though no one would put Ivan Ilych in the same league as Victor Frankenstein, he too, in his own way, is no less a monster. In the words of Augustine, he is *incurvatus in se*, or completely curved in on himself. As a result, he is unable even to recognize the people around him, let alone feel anything for them.

We can gain insight into *The Death of Ivan Ilych* through another great novella Tolstoy wrote late in his life, *Master and Man*. That tale focuses on Vasili Andree-vich Brekhunov, an up-and-coming landowner with a young family who dreams of becoming a millionaire. Lured by the prospect of a highly profitable business transaction, he and a servant he despises hastily embark on an ill-advised trek through a blizzard, intending to complete the purchase of a forest before competitors can arrive on the scene. Losing his way in the storm, it dawns on him that in such a predicament the millions he so longs for can do nothing for him. He eventually realizes that the life he has been living—focused purely on his own profit—means nothing. In the end, he lays down his life to protect his poor servant from the cold. He is dead, but at least for once in his life, he has lived.

Leo Tolstoy

Count Leo Tolstoy (1828–1910) was born into the landed nobility, but his parents died when he was young. He proved to be a rather desultory young man who left university, accumulated heavy gambling debts, and enlisted in the army, where he fought in the Caucasus, the setting of his last great work, *Hadji Murad*.

He married the daughter of a court physician, Sophia (known as Sonya), who was sixteen years his junior. On the eve of the wedding ceremony, Tolstoy gave Sonya his diaries, in which he detailed his many affairs and revealed that he had fathered a child by one of his serfs. Despite this, Sonya remained devoted to her husband for many years. She bore him fourteen children, eight of whom survived to adulthood. In addition to bearing and rearing their children, she also served as his secretary, copying by hand numerous drafts of the massive manuscript of *War and Peace*. Though highly fecund, the Tolstoys' marriage appears not to have remained happy.

As the decades passed, Tolstoy's philosophical and religious views evolved to such an extent that he decided to renounce both his inherited wealth and the copyrights to his literary works, a plan with which Sonya strongly disagreed. At the end of his life, Tolstoy sneaked away from his estate in the dead of night and died shortly thereafter, at the age of eighty-two, surrounded by representatives of the world press in a remote railroad station. In addition to his epochal literary endeavors—two of his novels, *War and Peace* and *Anna Karenina*, are routinely listed among the greatest ever written—Tolstoy also wrote extensively on theology and pacifism and founded a number of schools on his estate for the education of peasants.

Tolstoy wrote *The Death of Ivan Ilych* in the 1880s, shortly after he converted to Christianity. Like Thomas Jefferson, Tolstoy produced his own version of the New Testament, based almost entirely on what he felt to be the authentic teachings of Jesus. He espoused what to many appeared to be a stripped-down version of the faith marked by a thoroughgoing pacifism, the rejection of wealth, and a deep distrust of institutional religion. Partly as a result, Tolstoy was excommunicated from the Russian Orthodox Church in 1901.

In the years following the completion of *The Death of Ivan Ilych*, Tolstoy's efforts at publication ran afoul of censors, but it was finally published in Geneva in 1886. Though Tolstoy was only in his fifties, he had known death intimately over the course of much of his life, including the loss of his parents, the deaths of many comrades with whom he had served in the military, and the loss of five of his children. Suffering so many deaths could be a great burden in a person's life, but it might also lead to crucial insights. Someone who has seen death firsthand so many times might gain a clearer sense of what life is all about.

Ivan Ilych

The Death of Ivan Ilych opens in the law courts, Ivan Ilych's professional home, where his friend from school days, Peter Ivanovich, has been reading the newspaper. In the midst of a conversation about a celebrated case, Peter Ivanovich looks up and abruptly announces, "Gentlemen, Ivan Ilych has died."

The fact that the men learn of the death of their colleague and friend from the newspaper hints at the less-than-intimate nature of their relationship, an impression that is magnified by their reactions to the news: "The first thought of each of the gentlemen was of the changes and promotions it might occasion among themselves and their acquaintances." One colleague relishes the prospect that he will get a promotion and a raise of 800 rubles a year, while another thinks that at last he can get his brother-in-law a transfer and bring to a stop his wife's complaints that he never does anything for her relations.

Two other thoughts go through the minds of each man. First, "It is he who is dead and not I." Ivan Ilych has made a mess of things by dying, but each of them is still alive, and they quickly persuade themselves that any lessons that might lurk behind the death do not apply to them. Those who knew Ivan Ilych best also reluctantly acknowledge that they must now "fulfill the very tiresome demands of propriety by attending the funeral service and paying a visit of condolence to the widow." So after dinner that evening, Peter Ivanovich "sacrifices his usual nap" and sets off to visit the bereaved widow. What he sees there reveals still more about the deceased man's life.

Peter Ivanovich enters the viewing room preoccupied with uncertainty about what he should do. Should he cross himself or bow? So he performs an awkward combination of both. Only after observing virtually everything in the room does he become aware of the faint odor of the decomposing body, which he approaches. He sees that the face bears "a reproach and a warning to the living," which seems "out of place, or at least not at all applicable to Peter Ivanovich." Sensing a certain discomfort rising within him, he hurriedly flees the room. He encounters a colleague who reminds him of their upcoming game of cards later that evening, but his escape is foiled when Ivan Ilych's wife comes out and invites everyone into the funeral service.

Before it begins, however, she ushers Peter Ivanovich into a drawing room filled with furniture and knick-knacks over which Ivan Ilych had busied himself during his life. Everything about the room is awkward—the sofa's springs yield spasmodically under Peter Ivanovich's weight, and the widow's black shawl catches on one of the tables. Though outwardly overwhelmed by grief, she is able to engage in a detailed discussion with the butler regarding the prices of plots in the cemetery, during which, noticing that Peter Ivanovich's cigarette ash is threatening to fall on the table, she quickly passes him an ashtray, saying, "I consider it an affectation to say that my grief prevents my attending to practical affairs." She then tells him of her husband's suffering and how he screamed incessantly for the last three days of his life. Her visitor's thoughts are led to places he would rather not visit:

> "Three days of frightful suffering and death! Why, that might suddenly, at any time, happen to me," [Peter Ivanovich] thought, and for a moment felt terrified. But—he did not himself know how—the customary reflection at once occurred to him that this had happened to Ivan Ilych and not to him, and that it should not and could not happen to him, and that to think that it could would be yielding to depressing influences which he ought not to do.... After which reflection Peter Ivanovich felt reassured, and began to ask with interest about the details of Ivan Ilych's death, as though death was an accident natural to Ivan Ilych but certainly not to himself.

After the widow relates more details of the dreadful sufferings Ivan Ilych had endured, which Peter Ivanovich learns about through descriptions of the effect those sufferings produced on her nerves, she finds it necessary to get down to business. She inquires whether she could obtain more money from the government on the occasion of her husband's death. She knows to the penny how much she has coming to her, but her concern is to find out whether she can extract something more.

Peter Ivanovich thinks this over, but after criticizing the government for its stinginess, he informs her that nothing more can be got. The widow sighs, reluctantly accepting his answer. She then immediately begins devising some means to get rid of her visitor. It isn't long before Peter Ivanovich makes his escape and sits down to his favorite card game.

These seemingly mundane details reveal something profound about a pathetic way of life that is dominated only by concerns for details that relate to selfish ends. This disturbing realization could be taken as a mere idiosyncrasy of nineteenth-century Russian aristocratic society, but perhaps it is also at work in our own time and place. One way of putting it would be this: Everyone in Ivan Ilych's world—including Ivan Ilych himself—stands in direct violation of Immanuel Kant's categorical imperative that we should always treat other people as ends in themselves and never as means only.

The people we meet in the opening of *The Death of Ivan Ilych* interact primarily for purposes of using one another: Peter Ivanovich and colleagues see Ivan Ilych's death as opening up a rung on the professional ladder, and Ivan Ilych's widow sees Peter Ivanovich as a means of extracting more money from the government. Everyone is using everyone else, and no one seems to care about anyone other than themselves.

On the occasions when something resembling real awareness of another person's humanity bubbles up to the surface of consciousness—the reproach Peter Ivanovich sees in the dead man's countenance, or his horror at the suffering that Ivan Ilych endured during the last days of his life—distractions appear that enable the characters to divert their attention from such frightening trains of thought. Each of Ivan Ilych's friends quickly persuades himself that what has happened—the alarming intrusion of mortality into the easy, comfortable routine of their lives—somehow doesn't apply to them, so they need not trouble themselves further about it. It requires only a short sleigh ride from the scene of the funeral for Peter Ivanovich to wipe all unpleasantness from his mind and merrily assume his place at the card table.

The real point of the story's opening is not that Peter Ivanovich and his social circle are violating some moral imperative, doing what they should not do or failing to do what they should. The real point is this: No one in the story is prepared to face the true meaning of Ivan Ilych's death.

The death of Ivan Ilych is not just the death of one person, but the death of every person. Lost on nearly everyone in the story is the lesson that to be human is to be mortal, and that death is no less natural and necessary a part of life than birth. Medicine has made great strides since the days of Ivan Ilych—the discovery of X-rays, antibiotics, cancer chemotherapy drugs, and so on—but despite such progress, the human mortality rate remains firmly fixed at 100 percent.

The problem with Ivan Ilych, as well as with every other member of his social set, is that he mistakes the rule for the exception. And everyone makes the same mistake, which hides from them both life itself and any possibility of finding true meaning in their lives.

Perhaps this is what Tolstoy means when, after relating the events of Ivan Ilych's funeral, he begins the second part of the story with this enigmatic line:

"Ivan Ilych's life had been most simple and most ordinary and therefore most terrible." The terror lies not in simplicity or ordinariness as such, but instead in the universality of the habit—so widely taken for granted that no one even notices it—of denying the truth about life.

Only in truth, no matter how terrible it might seem at first, can we live authentic lives. But rather than face the truth, Ivan Ilych and his friends would rather keep wallowing in familiar falsehoods, supposing that they are somehow different from everyone else. We can express their thoughts for them: "Of course others must die," they think, "after all, they are mortal. And sometimes their deaths take a particularly disturbing form. But what can this business of death have to do with me? After all, I am different—special—and I need not concern myself with such unpleasantness. The fact that others must die, and that their deaths oblige me to observe the tiresome demands of propriety—that is unfortunate. But I am above it all, and this is ultimately no concern of mine."

Marriage

To gain some sense of the magnitude of the inauthenticity into which Ivan Ilych and his circle have stumbled, consider the story of his courtship and marriage. Ivan Ilych has been rapidly climbing the ladder of success. He has completed his law studies, obtained positions of increasing authority and prestige, and developed his own legal modus operandi, a habit of "eliminating all considerations irrelevant to the legal aspect of a case, and reducing even the most complicated case to a form in which it would be presented on paper only in its externals, completely excluding his personal opinion of the matter, while above all observing every prescribed formality."

Promoted yet again, Ivan Ilych takes up the position of examining magistrate in a new town. There, he meets his future wife, Praskovya Fedorovna Mikhel, "who was the most attractive, clever, and brilliant girl of the set in which he moved, and among other amusements and relaxations from his labors as examining magistrate, Ivan Ilych established light and playful relations with her." In his new and elevated post, he dances less frequently than he used to, but he still dances occasionally just to prove that he can do it better than most people. So at the end of an evening he sometimes danced with her, and "it was during these dances that he captivated her. She fell in love with him. Ivan Ilych had at first no definite intention of marrying, but when the girl fell in love with him, he said to himself, 'Really, why shouldn't I marry?'"

Ivan Ilych weighs the decision to marry much as he might tally up the arguments in a legal case: "She came of a good family, was not bad looking, and had some little property. He could have aspired to a more brilliant match, but even this was good. He had his salary, and she, he hoped, would have an equal income. She was well connected, and was a sweet, pretty, and thoroughly correct young woman."

Here we reach the crux of Ivan Ilych's decision to marry: "To say that Ivan Ilych married because he fell in love with Praskovya Fedorovna and found that she sympathized with his views of life would be as incorrect as to say that he married because his social circle approved of the match. He was swayed by both these considerations: the marriage gave him personal satisfaction, and at the same time it was considered the right thing by the most highly placed of his associates. So Ivan Ilych got married."

Love is conspicuously absent in Ivan Ilych's martial deliberations. Some might argue that this reflects the very different place and time in which the story is set, a culture operating with different notions about the proper basis for a marriage. Others might say that Ivan Ilych is simply doing what every prospective groom should do—setting aside desire and dispassionately weighing the decision on purely practical grounds. But in fact, Ivan Ilych does not love his bride. She has fallen in love with him under false pretenses, in the midst of dances for which Ivan Ilych cares not at all and to which he devotes himself only to prove that he is better than everyone else.

Ivan Ilych's reasons for getting married are all about the trappings of success—what other people will approve of and whether such a marriage will advance his career. He married her, in other words, because he could not see any sufficient countervailing reasons not to. When it comes to his marriage, Ivan Ilych is a stranger, someone unfamiliar with—and perhaps even alienated from—both the sacrament and his spouse. He treats the whole thing in a calculating fashion; his head is in it, but his heart is not. It is as though he is striking a bargain or arbitrating a legal dispute.

That something is seriously amiss is this marriage is confirmed in the following words: "The preparations for marriage and the beginning of married life, with its conjugal caresses, the new furniture, new crockery, and new linen were very pleasant until his wife became pregnant—so that Ivan Ilych had begun to think that marriage would not impair the easy, agreeable, gay and always decorous character of his life, approved of by society and regarded by himself as natural, but would even improve it." Note that "conjugal caresses" appear in a list of marital benefits that also includes new furniture, crockery, and linen. Ivan Ilych is merely furnishing his life—nothing more. He wants to perpetuate an existence committed to nothing but success, and this is precisely what he succeeds in doing.

Once his wife becomes pregnant, Ivan Ilych notices something "unpleasant, depressing, and unseemly" intruding upon his life. Suddenly she begins to be jealous and expects him to devote his whole attention to her. She expects him to share her excitement and anticipation, to feel closer to her than before and to join with her in planning for their new life as parents. She begins to make scenes. Ivan Ilych realizes, to his surprise, that "matrimony—at any rate with Praskovya Fedorovna—was not always conducive to the pleasures and amenities of life, but on the contrary often infringed both comfort and propriety, and that he must therefore entrench himself against such infringement." He begins seeking some means of "securing his independence," a need that only intensifies with the arrival of their child, which brings a whole new set of responsibilities "in which Ivan Ilych's sympathy was demanded but about which he understood nothing."

Ivan Ilych regards his wife's expectations and the needs of the child as an encroachment on his personal liberties and prerogatives. Like a good lawyer, he strives always to give up no more than he must. His marriage has presented him with demands that he did not foresee, and he feels cheated, as though a legal opponent had kept hidden from him important facts that should have been disclosed.

The key word here is "independence." In everything, Ivan Ilych is devoted to nothing more than his own liberty. He wants nothing to tie him down or constrain him in any way. Every human relationship threatens to do so, so he holds himself apart from everything and everyone—not just in judging those who come before him in the law courts, but even in what some might expect to be the deepest and most intimate circles of his personal life.

Simply put, Ivan Ilych is for no one but himself, and as a result, he can be with no one else. He is always alone. In every interaction, his first and only concern is, "What is convenient or advantageous to me, and what must I do to achieve the outcome I desire?" He is completely curved in on himself.

Work

Consider Ivan Ilych's true feelings toward his profession, which are revealed in the "hardest year of his life." This occurs seventeen years after his marriage. Ivan Ilych realizes that his salary is insufficient and that he has been forgotten by those he had been expecting to advance his career. Others find his situation quite ordinary and even fortunate, but Ivan knows that something is deeply wrong.

After a sleepless night, he resolves to travel to St. Petersburg and obtain a post that pays 5,000 rubles a year. He does not care what department he works in or even what sort of work he does—only that it carry a salary of 5,000 rubles. During his train journey, Ivan Ilych unexpectedly learns that personnel have shifted in his former department, and he ends up receiving a promotion with his desired salary. Suddenly his ill humor vanishes and he is "completely happy."

There are multiple ironies here. First, we see more clearly than ever that Ivan Ilych does not really care about his work, except for the income it provides. The nature of the work is of no importance to him. He is not a professional—someone professing a calling beyond himself and therefore serving a greater purpose—but merely a job holder, who regards work as little more than a means to make money. If offered a higher-paying position, he would take it in a heartbeat.

Second, to make Ivan Ilych "completely happy" takes nothing more than a raise, as though money alone can buy happiness. The fact that a mere boost in income leads Ivan Ilych to suppose himself happy is a sign that he is traveling down the wrong path. We know him well enough by this point not to be at all surprised when he soon realizes that even his coveted salary of 5,000 rubles is not enough.

Illness

A still greater sign that Ivan Ilych is traveling the wrong path is provided by the illness he contracts and his reaction to it. Dying can be difficult, but it is infinitely more difficult to die alone. One day while showing the draper how to hang curtains, Ivan Ilych slips from the ladder and knocks his side. Over time, he develops a worsening pain there, senses a strange taste in his mouth, and loses his appetite.

It becomes apparent that Ivan Ilych is suffering from a rather serious illness, and a series of doctors are called in to render a diagnosis and recommend an appropriate course of therapy. There is the usual waiting and the usual important air assumed by the doctors, that "if only you put yourself in our hands we will arrange everything." Ivan Ilych soon realizes they are treating him just the same as he is accustomed to treating accused people in the law courts.

In a nod to the biblical injunction "judge not, lest you be judged," Ivan Ilych now finds himself in the position of the accused. Contrary to his lifelong presumption, he discovers that he is no longer in charge of his own fate. And he realizes that the doctors' diagnoses—a floating kidney, a chronic catarrh, or appendicitis—have nothing to do with what he is experiencing. The doctors won't even tell him whether the condition is serious. In response to such questions, one doctor simply peers at him "sternly over his spectacles with one eye, as if to say, 'Prisoner, if you will not keep to the questions put to you, I shall be obliged to have you removed from the court.'" The doctors adopt a professional posture much like Ivan Ilych's, eliminating all human considerations from the case.

Soon Ivan Ilych's life changes dramatically. He finds himself becoming increasingly distracted at work and having difficulty attending to cases. At his beloved card games, his mind wanders, and he misses out on a grand slam. He senses that he is living on the brink of an abyss, yet no one else seems to understand or pity him.

After some time his wife's brother comes for a visit. Catching sight of Ivan Ilych for the first time in a long time, his brother-in-law's gaze says everything—he opens his mouth to utter an exclamation of surprise but checks himself. No one will tell Ivan Ilych the truth, but his brother-in-law's stare tells him all he needs to know. Later the man tells his sister: "Why he's a dead man! Look at his eyes—there's no life left in them."

The reality of death begins to sink in, as Ivan Ilych thinks to himself: "Death. Yes, death. And none of them knows or wishes to know it, and they have no pity for me. . . . It's all the same to them, but they will die too! Fools! I first, and they later, but it will be the same for them. And now they are merry . . . the beasts!" Again, the irony is palpable. Contemplating the prospect of his own death, Ivan Ilych feels utterly alone and ignored. He wallows in self-pity. In fact, however, Ivan Ilych would no doubt have reacted in just the same way had it been his brother-in-law or one of his colleagues who developed such an illness. Ivan Ilych would have protected himself from any unpleasantness by hovering at a comfortable distance, not allowing himself to be swept up by any depressing influences.

As Ivan Ilych's health declines, his musings are drawn back to his school days, and he recalls the syllogism he had learned in logic: Caius is a man, men are mortal, therefore Caius is mortal. "It had always seemed to him correct as applied to Caius, but certainly not as applied to himself. That Caius—man in the abstract—was mortal, was perfectly correct, but he was not Caius, not an abstract man, but a creature quite, quite separate from all the others." This, of course, is the core of Ivan Ilych's misalignment in life—the same misalignment that afflicts every other member of his social circle. He has supposed that, despite a great deal of evidence to the contrary, he is somehow separate from everyone else, apart from and above the rest of humanity. This has caused him to live as though he were immortal and has prevented him from enjoying any real human fellowship.

Ivan Ilych must live with the desolation of a man on whom the realization is dawning that everything he has lived for has been false. The further he progressed down the path of success, the more removed he became from everyone else. With each step he became more entangled in a web of falsity and deceit.

In Ivan Ilych's world, no one ever faces the truth. No one is prepared to consider the dreadful possibility that someday their comfortable lives will end and that all the trappings of success in life—money, power, prestige, and the like—will turn out to be hollow and meaningless. Ivan Ilych comes to believe that he lost his life over hanging curtains—merely decorating his life when he should have been furnishing it with something real.

Several things torment Ivan Ilych above all. One is the deception—"the lie, which for some reason they all accepted, that he was not dying but was simply ill, and that he only need keep quiet and undergo a treatment and then something very good would result." He wants to call out, "Stop lying! You know and I know that I am dying," but he doesn't.

He also suffers because no one pities him as he wishes to be pitied. He longs to be petted and comforted like a child, but he also knows that "he is an important functionary, with a beard turning grey, and that therefore what he longs for is impossible."

What torments him above all, however, is the fear contained in a question: "What if I did not live as I ought to have done?" But as soon as this terrible idea occurs to him, he dismisses it: "How could that be, when I did everything properly?" Nonetheless, as time goes on, the impossible becomes possible: "It occurred to him that his scarcely perceptible attempts to struggle against what was considered good by the most highly placed people, those scarcely noticeable impulses which he had immediately suppressed, might have been the real thing, and all the rest false."

Feeling so trapped in a web of falsity that he has no hope of extricating himself—that everything he has lived for has been falsehood and deception, hiding life and death from him—Ivan Ilych gives in to his wife's desire that he take communion. Afterward, all he can say to her and everyone else is, "Go away! Go away and leave me alone!" Even in his isolation, Ivan Ilych craves nothing so much as solitude.

Death

As long as we live in denial, unable to face up to the fact that mortality is written into the very fabric of our being, we are certain to find ourselves leading false lives. And this, not cancer, turns out to be Ivan Ilych's greatest affliction. The tale of *The Death of Ivan Ilych* suggests that as long as we flee from our mortality, we remain locked in solitary confinement, unable to see—let alone to care for—anyone else. Only when we recognize in the souls of others the very same alloy as our own can we hope to find genuine fellowship. Only by facing death is any measure of transcendence possible for us in life.

The scene of Ivan Ilych's death is marked by what many critics regard as a deus ex machina, a nasty, eleventh-hour literary trick. Ivan Ilych wails for three whole days, so loudly that he can be heard even through two closed doors; but then, his hand falls on his son's head. The boy catches it, presses it to his lips, and begins to cry. Suddenly, Ivan Ilych catches sight of the light. He looks at his son and feels sorry for him. He looks at his wife and feels sorry for her, too. For the first time in his adult life—at the very moment of his dying, no less—Ivan Ilych discovers his capacity to see his life from someone else's perspective, and even to feel for them. Suddenly, death is no more, and in place of it there is only light. His dying goes on for two more hours, but then, at last, he stretches out and dies.

This sequence of events reveals the true meaning of *The Death of Ivan Ilych*, and it is no trick. Ivan Ilych dies not in the last month, week, day, or minute of his life, but throughout his life, and the pace of his dying increases the longer he lives. With increasing vigor and resolution, he ignores the intimations of his own mortality, pretending instead that he can keep heaping up wealth and prestige forever.

Yet in living increasingly only for himself, he becomes more and more cut off from others, to the point that he constructs a prison cell for himself, from which he serves out his self-imposed sentence of solitary confinement. Only at the end, seeing as if for the first time the tear-stained faces of his son and wife, does he discover a new possibility, a new way of being with and for others.

Here lies a deep insight concerning generosity and the spirit of giving. It is only when we feel ourselves being with and for others that genuine fellow feeling and the generosity to which it can give birth become possible. As long as we keep ourselves apart, treating others as mere means and sucking everything and everyone into ourselves like a human version of a black hole, genuine compassion is impossible.

For virtually all of Ivan Ilych's life, he served no one. He never truly lived. Instead, he spent his days allowing the life to drain out of himself. But in the last hours of his life, and even in his most debilitated state, he discovers the possibility of serving others. He can relieve their suffering by dying. Only at this moment does the specter of death vanish from view. It is in dying that Ivan Ilych finds life.

three

ALBERT
Service to the Suffering

THERE ARE MANY WAYS TO TAKE THE MEASURE OF A HUMAN LIFE, addressing the question, "What has this person's life amounted to?" One is by sheer length. The Bible's Methuselah famously lived 969 years. On a less spectacular scale, the philosopher Plato lived to be 80, statesman Winston Churchill to 90, and the artist Grandma Moses to 101. Such long lives seem complete, if not necessarily full.

By contrast, lives cut short evoke a sense of lost potential. Consider the death of the painter Vincent Van Gogh at age 37, composer Wolfgang Mozart at 35, or poet Percy Bysshe Shelley at 29. Scholars will speculate for a long time about the great works they might have produced had they been able to work and create to an old age.

Which is preferable? To be a candle that burns brightly for only a short time, or to burn less intensely for a much longer time? This is the choice facing Achilles in Homer's *Iliad*. He could remain at Troy and cement his reputation as the greatest warrior among the Greeks, ensuring that his story will be celebrated through the ages, or he could go back home and lead a long but relatively undistinguished life among his people. He opts for the former.

Few of us ever confront such a choice directly, but it does introduce another standard by which a life can be assayed—namely, fame. Can we take the measure of a person's life by the number of times his or her name or face appears in the newspapers or on television, or the number of books he or she might have written? Were the Greeks correct in supposing that such notoriety is a form of immortality, allowing those whose words and deeds are preserved beyond their own generation to cheat death and live on in the minds and hearts of others?

This suggestion is problematic in part because fame does not distinguish between different kinds of lives we might label as admirable or disreputable. Some people achieve great fame because they are important benefactors to humankind—artists, politicians, and inventors—but others achieve an equal degree of fame because of the harm they have wreaked on humankind—despots, mass murderers, and other malefactors. Fame isn't the same in both cases. Who would not prefer that their children and grandchildren live out their lives in obscurity rather than achieve fame through misdeeds?

Another way to take the measure of a life is wealth. Can the value of a life be assessed by the riches a person has accumulated? In our day, this suggestion has the ring of plausibility. The very rich receive a great deal of attention. We have an immense appetite for stories about how the rich got richer, how they are continuing to do so, and what they are doing with their riches, whether spending them or giving them away. The words and actions of some people are treated as more significant than those of others simply because they have more money.

By this standard, John D. Rockefeller, who has been pegged as the richest American ever, and perhaps even the richest person ever, amounted to more than anyone else. By this standard, those with the most money lead the most momentous lives.

But here, too, difficulties arise. Some rich people did not make their money by their own devices. Instead, they inherited it, married into it, or came upon it by sheer luck. Others achieved wealth by frankly nefarious means. The quest for wealth led some to damage the lives of other people by promoting vices such as gambling and prostitution. Still others acquired their wealth through intimidation and brute force.

Socrates seems to have believed that no amount of wealth can adequately compensate a person for going through life with a corrupt character—being greedy, cowardly, intemperate, or prideful. For one thing, a bad character makes it difficult or even impossible to make good use of wealth. If people are not good to begin with, merely handing them a lot of money may make them even worse, by providing them with greater wherewithal to satisfy their corrupt desires. Having great wealth might lead such a person to a life of idle self-indulgence and debauchery, encouraging him or her to satisfy baser and baser impulses. Such a life is not fit for a human being, Socrates might say, because it makes it all but impossible to express what is best in humanity.

A similar point applies to another means of taking a life's measure: power. Some people might suppose that the powerful lead the most momentous lives because their decisions affect the most people. A boss hires and fires underlings, which seems to make the boss's life the more important of the two. Whenever people rise above others in a hierarchy—whether in the military, the corporate world, or politics—we tend to think more highly of them. History, after all, is written primarily about generals, CEOs, and presidents and far less about privates, entry-level employees, and ordinary citizens.

Again, however, there are problems with saying that power is the parameter by which to assess a life. People who wield power might hold it justly, by the consent of those for whom they are responsible, but power can also be acquired and held unjustly. Some tyrants and despots attain power by force, eliminating anyone who stands in their way. No one of good character would wish their child or grandchild to become a usurper.

In addition, power can be used for evil purposes as well as for good. Some people exert influence with wisdom, moderation, and compassion, while others use it primarily to advance their own selfish ambitions. The very possession of it has a tendency to damage the character of those who wield it; as Lord Acton famously said, "Power tends to corrupt, and absolute power to corrupt absolutely." When fallible human beings no longer need trouble themselves about what others think of their words and actions, their worst often comes to the fore.

Christina

Consider the case of Christina Onassis (1950–1988), who seemed to "have it all"—fame, wealth, and power. Her father, Aristotle Socrates Onassis, had risen from humble circumstances to become owner of the world's largest privately held shipping fleet and one of the world's most famous, wealthy, and powerful businessmen. Christina was raised in the lap of luxury and had everything that money could buy. Her dolls reportedly sported dresses by the French designer Christian Dior, and she rode ponies presented to her by a Saudi king.

Yet none of this could not make Christina happy. For one thing, her family life was filled with misfortune. Her father fell in love with the opera singer Maria Callas, and her parents divorced when she was nine. This affair with Callas was a great embarrassment to the family. Later, Christina strongly disapproved of her father's 1968 marriage to Jacqueline Kennedy, widow of the late US president. Then in 1973, her brother, Alexander, died in a plane crash. The next year her mother died of a suspected drug overdose, and in 1975 her father also died.

Christina suffered her own marital difficulties. She married four times. Her first marriage lasted only nine months; her second, fourteen months; and her third, seventeen months. Her final marriage to a French pharmaceutical heir lasted three years and produced a daughter, Athina.

Throughout her adult life, Christina ranked as one of the world's most famous women. She was a staple of the tabloid press, which regularly carried stories of her stormy personal life. Upon inheriting 55 percent of her father's business empire at the age of twenty-four, she also became one of the world's richest women, and her lavish spending habits were the frequent topic of gossip. Finally, she enjoyed immense power as her father's anointed successor, successfully operating his far-flung interests after his death.

Yet by most accounts, Christina was not happy. Her stepsister once said that she moved from relationship to relationship, relying on each new one to forget the pain of the last one. Some speculated that Christina was seeking a substitute for the affection of a father who rarely devoted time to her when she was a child. Many who knew her said she was desperately afraid of being alone.

In her twenties, Christina battled drug dependency, as well as an eating disorder. Having so much money meant that people were always eager to latch on to her, undercutting her efforts to build a normal family and lead a normal life. Said her stepsister, "She had houses all over the world, but never really a home." When her father died, Christina lamented, "I am all alone in the world now."

Christina Onassis died at the age of only thirty-seven. If fame, wealth, and power are key sources of happiness, then she should have been one of the happiest women in the world. Yet her life seems to have been marked by an inability to find any enduring source of acceptance and love. The only exception may have been her daughter, who was left motherless at the age of three.

In reflecting on the role of wealth in her life, Christina once said, "Happiness is not based on money. And the best proof of this is our family." On another occasion, she is reported to have said, "Sometimes when you have everything, you can't really tell what matters." In short, many of the conventional measures of a life—the ones most frequently reflected in the pages of glossy magazines—turn out to provide a less-than-reliable standard by which to determine what a life has amounted to. Some famous, rich, and powerful people seem to be leading relatively good lives, yet many others serve as notable examples of how base desires express themselves when freed of constraints.

Most of us know good and admirable people whose lives are largely devoid of fame, fortune, and influence. Many virtuous people have never appeared in the popular media, accumulated wealth, or acquired the power to hire and fire anyone, yet their lives are in many respects exemplary. We do not often hear of such people, at least through the same channels that transmit the stories of the famous, rich, and powerful, but they are in our midst, making a difference every day. Some are schoolteachers. Others are religious leaders. Others are volunteers who serve in shelters, teach Sunday school, coach youth sports teams, and simply do the best they can parenting their children and caring for family members and loved ones.

What such good people lack in conventional measures of success they more than make up for in the clarity of their vision of a worthy life and their efforts to aid and enrich the lives of others. These unsung heroes are not world-historical figures, titans of industry, or conquerors; they are just good human beings who, in one way or another, have devoted their lives to serving others instead of merely themselves. In living for something beyond self, they help us to see more deeply what a good life is really all about.

Albert Schweitzer

One widely known example of someone who served others is Albert Schweitzer, the Alsatian polymath who became one of the most admired figures of the twentieth century. There is a danger in focusing on a man such as Schweitzer precisely because he became so famous. His example may suggest that even a life devoted to service should be judged in part by the amount of attention, money, and influence such a person manages to attract. Yet Schweitzer himself would have been the first to say that a servant who labors in obscurity, poverty, and powerlessness may lead the most admirable life.

The reason for focusing on Schweitzer is not the fact that his service attracted a great deal of attention. Instead, the reason is his deep intellect and character and the fact that he thought and wrote so powerfully about the meaning of service. Schweitzer was not always the most effective servant, but he was one of the most articulate and inspiring writers on the subject of service. In this sense, he presents a particularly good opportunity for understanding where a life devoted to service might come from, and what sort of vision might guide such a person from day to day.

By almost any standard, Albert Schweitzer was a great man. In the domain of music, he produced highly influential scholarly works on Johann Sebastian Bach, helped to develop new standards for organ building, and achieved worldwide renown as an organist. As a theologian, he authored groundbreaking studies on the historical Jesus and the mysticism of Saint Paul. As a philosopher, he developed the idea that reverence for life should be regarded as humanity's defining principle. And as a physician, he founded and spent the better part of fifty years working in a missionary hospital in what is now Gabon in west central Africa.

In recognition of his philosophy of reverence for life as expressed through his work as a medical missionary, Schweitzer received the 1952 Nobel Peace Prize. The story of Schweitzer's life, and in particular his calling to medical mission work, provides deep insights into what it means to serve.

It is important to acknowledge at the outset that Schweitzer, though a great man, was not a perfect one. For one thing, he was not steadfast in his Christian faith. During the last decades of his life, he seems to have become almost agnostic as regards the God of Christianity, moving toward more universal ethical principles. In addition, many visitors to his African mission hospital criticized the medical care being provided there as antiquated and thought that philanthropic donations were not being put to the best possible use. Finally, although Schweitzer spent decades in Africa, he never acquired more than a rudimentary understanding of native languages, did not integrate himself into the local cultures, and did little to train local people to provide their own medical care—all goals that are today considered essential to international humanitarian work.

Despite such shortcomings, Schweitzer was nonetheless one the best-known and most-admired people of the twentieth century. Winston Churchill called him "a genius of humanity."

Born in 1875 in the Alsace-Lorraine region along the long-disputed border between France and Germany, Schweitzer was the son of an evangelical pastor whose medieval church served both Catholic and Protestant congregations. After completing his secondary education, the young Schweitzer studied the organ for eight years, followed by theological studies and a term of compulsory military service. In 1899 he published his dissertation on the religious philosophy of Immanuel Kant.

In 1905, at the age of thirty, Schweitzer answered a call from Paris for medical missionaries by enrolling in medical school, eventually completing his studies in 1911. Before that, he had been serving as the principal of a theological school. In 1906, he published a work on the historical Jesus, emphasizing Christianity's origin as a Jewish apocalyptic movement. In 1912, he and his wife, Helene, used their own money to organize a medical mission to Africa, where a year later they converted an old henhouse into a hospital.

With the outbreak of World War I, Schweitzer and Helene, who were Germans working in a French colony, were placed under the supervision of the French military, and then after four years they were transported to France for health reasons. In 1918, Schweitzer reclaimed his parents' French citizenship and began raising money through lectures and organ performances to return to Africa. In 1924, he did so with a small staff of health professionals who built a new and larger hospital around which a village, Lambaréné, developed and grew.

Except for relatively short visits to Europe and the United States, Schweitzer spent the rest of his life there, including the entirety of World War II. He functioned primarily as a physician but also helped to run the village and continued his scholarly research and writing. When he received the Nobel Peace Prize in 1952, he used the award money to found a leprosarium there. Schweitzer died in 1965 at the age of ninety and is buried overlooking the river that runs along the village he founded.

When Albert Schweitzer speaks to the worthiness to serve the suffering, there are many reasons to listen carefully. In addition to being a great thinker and writer on the topic, Schweitzer was also a man of action who put his principles into practice. He turned away from the ease and security of his university post, the lecture circuit, and the concert halls of Europe to serve obscure people in a remote and potentially hazardous part of the world where his personal health, and that of his wife, suffered.

He did so not with funds from a government or a large multinational philanthropic organization but his own money, and he continued to work tirelessly to raise funds to support his mission for the rest of his life. In short, Schweitzer not only espoused the importance of service, he actually lived it, day in and day out, for decades. What, then, did Albert Schweitzer have to say about serving the suffering?

In the final chapter of his 1922 book *On the Edge of the Primeval Forest*, Schweitzer presents his views on service to the suffering. He opens his account with a vivid image. In 1917, he and his exhausted wife, who have been operating their inland hospital for more than four years, have just arrived at the mouth of the Ogowe River to spend the warm, rainy months at the seaside. He is exploring the abandoned huts around the house in which they will be living, when, opening the door of the last one,

I saw a man lying on the ground with his head almost buried in the sand and ants running all over him. It was a victim of sleeping sickness whom his companions had left there, probably some days before, because they could not take him any further. He was past all help, though he still breathed. While I was busied with him I could see through the door of the hut the bright blue waters of the bay in their frame of green woods, a scene of almost magic beauty, looking still more enchanting in the flood of golden light poured over it by the setting sun. To be shown in a single glance such a paradise and such a helpless, hopeless, misery, was overwhelming. . . . But it was a symbol of the condition of Africa.

In this brief account, Schweitzer displays the soul of a poet. The unconscious man is overrun with ants. He has been abandoned by his companions; he is "past all help." And yet, Schweitzer reveals in a subordinate clause, he immediately busies himself with him. The fact that this victim of sleeping sickness is "hopeless" does not diminish Schweitzer's commitment to care for him, and it is precisely through the act of serving that he becomes aware of a wondrous sight outside his door, a scene of great, "almost magic" beauty.

The juxtaposition of the hopelessness of a moribund human being and the blue waters of the bay illuminated by the golden light of the setting sun conveys Schweitzer's essential message: A commitment to action is an essential aspect of worthiness, as embodied in his famous declaration, "My life is my argument." If this is true, stories may offer more important insights on the aspiration to serve than any ethical principles or moral exhortations.

Schweitzer's writings are full of such stories. As a child, he modeled his prayers on those of his mother, but instead of just praying for human beings, he included "all things that have breath." Because his father was a Lutheran pastor, he came from more privileged circumstances than many of his classmates, but his sense of justice prevented him from wearing nicer clothes than they. He could not accept privileges for himself that had been denied to others. Since others had no overcoat, he wore none. Because others' mittens had no fingers, his mittens lacked them as well.

By age twenty-one Schweitzer had resolved that when he turned thirty he would devote himself entirely to following in the footsteps of Christ. "Jesus had simply taken me prisoner since my childhood," he wrote. "My going to Africa was an act of obedience to Jesus." Schweitzer could not just reflect on principles such as justice, equality, and sacrifice. He had to live them.

Upon his return to Lambaréné, he finds locals being pressed into military service for the Cameroons. Many of them had contracted dysentery. As these unfortunate souls were being loaded onto a steamer, the natives "began to experience what war really is." The vessel's departure is accompanied by the wailing of women, and it is only after its trail of smoke disappears in the distance that the crowd begins to disperse.

But on the side of the riverbank sits an old woman whose son has been taken. She is weeping silently. Schweitzer sits down beside her, taking her hand in an effort to comfort her. She continues crying as if she does not notice him. "Suddenly," writes Schweitzer, "I felt that I was crying with her, silently, toward the setting sun, as she was."

This story illustrates that serving the suffering means being willing to suffer with, not just to minister to, those in pain. In his memoirs Schweitzer writes: "Whoever is spared personal pain must feel himself called to help in diminishing the pain of others. We must all carry our share of the misery that lies upon the world."

Schweitzer's time in Gabon was contemporaneous with both the First and Second World Wars. He recognized that to the endemic scourges of dysentery, leprosy, malaria, sand fleas, sleeping sickness, yaws, and other diseases he saw at the hospital were being added the scourges of warfare. Infectious microorganisms were not the only things killing human beings. Human beings themselves represented one of the greatest sources of their own suffering.

Schweitzer could administer medications and apply dressings to treat infections, but when it came to the tide of warfare, he could only stand by and watch as local men were impressed. To the old woman whose son had been conscripted he could offer little more than his own tears, which she seemed not even to notice. Off in the distance glows the breathtaking yet utterly impassive setting sun.

At about the same time, Schweitzer reads a magazine article declaring that there will always be wars—a manifestation, so its author claims, of a noble thirst for glory in every human heart. From Schweitzer's point of view, however, such sentiments are born of ignorance. The apologists for war, he says, "would reconsider their opinions if they spent a day in one of the African theatres of war, walking along the paths in the virgin forest between lines of corpses of carriers who had sunk under their load and found a solitary death by the roadside, and if, with these innocent and unwilling victims before them, they were to meditate in the gloomy stillness of the forest on war as it really is."

Again, juxtaposition provides the key to insight. It is at the border of the primeval forest, between bustling civilization and peaceful nature, between "lines of corpses" and the forest's "gloomy stillness," that human beings are most likely to see war for what it really is. Row upon row of corpses tell the tale less well than a solitary death. Truth, in other words, is most perceptible in certain places—places that armchair philosophers and cabinet-room politicians need to encounter if they are to stand a chance of discerning what is really going on.

Time and again Schweitzer had been told that the primitive peoples of Africa do not suffer, do not experience pain, in the same way as Europeans. They are "never so ill as we are, and do not feel so much pain," Europeans argued. But after four and a half years at the edge of the primeval forest, Schweitzer knows that the local people suffer the same diseases as the Europeans, that they are "subject to the power of that terrible lord whose name is Pain."

Whether the news media tell us about it or not, Schweitzer says, millions and millions of people suffer every day from conditions that medical science can avert.

He argues that coming to the aid of such people is a natural response of the sympathy that "Jesus and religion generally call for," but it is also dictated by "our most fundamental ideas and reasonings." It is a matter not just of "good work," but of a duty "that must not be shirked."

From Schweitzer's point of view, the arrival of professed followers of Jesus has not been a blessing to such peoples. In fact, it has meant that some peoples have died out, that others are in the process of dying out, and that the conditions of others are worsening. From his point of view, European civilization, he writes, is burdened with a great debt: "Anything we give them is not benevolence but atonement. For every one who scattered injury someone ought to go out to take help, and when we have done all that is in our power, we shall not have atoned for the thousandth part of our guilt." This work of atonement cannot be the sole province of governments, Schweitzer argues, because governments can do only what society is already convinced needs to be done. No government can discharge the duties of humanitarianism, a responsibility that rests primarily with communities and individuals.

Here Schweitzer issues a special call to the medical profession, including those who aspire to be physicians: "We must have doctors who go out among the colored people of their own accord and are ready to put up with all that is meant by absences from home and civilization." While the prospect may not appear enticing, particularly to children of privilege in the richer parts of the world, "I can say from experience that they will find a rich reward for all that they renounce in the good that they can do."

At this point Schweitzer introduces his most essential and transformative idea, which he calls, "the Fellowship of those who bear the Mark of Pain." Its members include those who have learned firsthand the meaning of physical pain and bodily anguish. These people, regardless of where they happen to be located around the world, are united by a "secret bond." They know "the horrors of suffering to which man can be exposed, and they know the longing to be free from pain."

> Those who have been delivered from such pain should not rejoice that they are free from it, but as people "whose eyes are now open," they should labor to bring to others the deliverance they have enjoyed. Someone who has, with a doctor's aid, recovered from a severe illness, should provide such help to another. A mother whose child has been saved should help to ensure that some other mother's child is spared. Those of us who have been comforted at the bedside of a dying loved one should ensure that others enjoy the same consolation.

One particularly noteworthy implication of Schweitzer's perspective concerns the role of experiencing suffering as a precondition for responding to the suffering of others. Schweitzer is not calling on everyone, but on those who have known suffering, as members of the "Fellowship of those who bear the Mark of Pain." More specifically, he is calling on those whose experience of suffering—either firsthand or through contact with others in pain—has been relieved through the efforts of others. Why? Part of the answer reflects the role suffering plays in opening our eyes, ears, and hearts to the travails of others.

Moreover, there is the matter of justice and duty. Schweitzer argues that people who have been helped by others should then take on the duty of helping others. Schweitzer's perspective represents a natural expression of the role of suffering in Christianity, a faith which holds that Jesus, the incarnation of God, suffered and died in perhaps the most agonizing manner possible, crucifixion. For Schweitzer as for Christianity, hope for each person and for humanity itself is to be found in and through the encounter with suffering.

Who is worthy to serve the suffering? As Schweitzer sees it, the answer is simple: anyone who has known suffering. Perhaps only a doctor can prescribe a curative medicine or perform a life-saving operation. And perhaps only a person of considerable wealth can afford to bankroll a foreign medical mission. But no one entirely lacks the means to do good. Whether through direct action or by supporting the efforts of others, every person can play a role in suffering's relief.

The principal limitations are not education and wealth, but imagination and conviction. And the time to act is now. "Truth," Schweitzer writes, "has no special time of its own. Its hour is now—always, and indeed then most truly when it seems most unsuitable to actual circumstances." What he is talking about here is not just a new aid-to-Africa program, but an awakening from a kind of thoughtlessness, "the calling into life" of "a new spirit of humanity."

Schweitzer anticipates an objection. Some will ask, "What good could it possibly do to cope with the misery of the world simply by sending a doctor here and another one there?" In other words, isn't the effort to banish pain and suffering from the face of the earth ultimately futile, inevitably ending in disappointment? To this Schweitzer responds that "even a single doctor with the most modest equipment means very much for very many."

No one should allow the fact that we cannot do everything to prevent us from attempting to do something. Though the recently ended First World War has made putting together such a mission more difficult and expensive than ever, Schweitzer resolves to continue his work by returning to the service of the suffering people he has written about:

> I have not lost courage. The misery I have seen gives me strength, and faith in my fellowmen supports my confidence in the future. I do hope that I shall find a sufficient number of people who, because they themselves have been saved from physical suffering, will respond to this request on behalf of those who are in similar need. . . . I do hope that among the doctors of the world there will be several besides myself who will be sent out, here or there, by "the Fellowship of those who bear the Mark of Pain."

Although the questions Schweitzer raises are eternal, he believes that each generation of human beings must confront them anew, that the conversation about life's purpose must be renewed with each generation and in the heart of every person. "Just as a tree bears year after year the same fruit, and yet fruit which is each year new," he writes, "so must all permanently valuable ideas be continually born again in thought."

For Schweitzer the ultimate question concerns not only worthiness to serve, but the very meaning of life. And it is a religious one: "In religion, we try to find the answer to the elementary question with which each of us is newly confronted every morning, namely, what meaning and what value is to be ascribed to our life? What am I in the world? What is my purpose in it? What may I hope for in this world?" It is our answers to these questions, Schweitzer believes, that enable us to serve the suffering.

The contrast between Christina Onassis and Albert Schweitzer could hardly be sharper. The former, born into one of the wealthiest families in the world, had everything money could buy. Her exploits were regularly featured on the front pages of tabloids worldwide. And she assumed control of one of the world's largest shipping empires. In conventional terms, she led a charmed life. And yet she was miserable. She could obtain everything she wanted, but this was precisely her problem. When we begin to focus our lives on what we want, we inevitably find ourselves wanting more and more. The satisfaction that comes with a new purchase, no matter the price tag, is always short-lived. Christina found herself caught in a vortex of discontent from which no amount of money, fame, or power could extricate her. She had forgotten—perhaps had never known—that we can never have enough of what we don't really need.

Albert Schweitzer, on the other hand, sought not to satisfy himself, but to serve others. Far from attempting to accumulate more and more money, fame, and power, Schweitzer laid down all he had to fund his missionary activities. Schweitzer was not at the center of his own universe. He sought not to make himself larger and larger, but to embed his life in service to a purpose far larger than himself.

To those convinced that life is about extracting as much as possible, Schweitzer's path in life can only seem nonsensical. Why would anyone possessed of such gifts forsake wealth, comfort, and fame for a life among the impoverished, under conditions that gradually sapped health and in a part of the world where even members of the media generally feared to tread? But As Schweitzer sees it, it makes perfect sense. We come to life not by tightening our stranglehold on everything we can grasp, but by extending our hands to help and share with others.

four

REBECCA
Service to Family

THE FAMILY MAY BE THE MOST NATURAL OF ALL CONTEXTS FOR SERVICE. Consider the following story. A small boy decides that he would like to earn some money, so be prepares a bill for his mother, in which he sets beside each of his household chores a certain sum of money for which he requests payment. His mother looks over the list, then hands him back another piece of paper. On it she has recorded acts of service such as carrying him in her womb for nine months, giving birth to him, nursing him when he was sick, and so on. Next to each service she has written, "No Charge." The boy looks this over and then hands his original bill back to her a second time, now with the words "Paid in Full" written across the bottom.

There is a biological basis for service in the family. We are born into a state of utter helplessness, unable to feed, clothe, shelter, and protect and sustain ourselves in any way. Day in and day out, for years and even decades, children depend on their parents for their survival. In addition, parents and grandparents do the work of humanizing the next generation, by sharing with them the gifts of language and culture that enable them to participate in human community and eventually to contribute to it in their own right. Without parents or their equivalent, the human species would vanish.

Infants are endowed with traits that endear them to other humans. The eyes, for example, take up an extra-large proportion of the face, a layout that most human beings find inherently cute. Infants' cries, though not pleasant, have the power to move the human heart, evoking compassion in those who hear.

Of course, family means more than just caring for helpless infants. Marriages join spouses in mutual dedication, even though neither depends on the other for survival. Again, biology offers at least a partial explanation. For the human species to survive and men and women to produce progeny, they must depend on each other to reproduce and rear offspring. Yet procreation is not the sole purpose of marriage. Many unions are childless, and children are not necessary for spouses to be devoted to one another throughout their lifetimes. Perhaps sharing our days with another person makes life more complete.

Some of the most remarkable examples of familial devotion occur when a family member suffers an injury or falls ill. I know parents who have dedicated their lives to caring for disabled children. In one case, the child, now a middle-aged adult, has cerebral palsy, and her mother spends every day tending to her needs. In another, the child had a severe chromosomal abnormality that was expected to end her life before she reached the age of one year, but her mother's assiduous care enabled her to live into her late teens. These parents never expected a biological return on their investment, such as grandchildren. Instead, they simply loved their children.

The same can happen in reverse. Many of us know adult children who have cut back on their work schedules and even taken leaves of absence or resigned their jobs in order to care for an ailing parent. The same happens with ailing spouses. Such people serve their relatives not because they must, but because they choose to. Some make the decision to seek professional help or place their loved ones in a long-term care facility, and few would gainsay these decisions. People make such choices all the time, at substantial personal sacrifice. But the fact that some opt not to take on care-taking burdens only magnifies the fact that it is a real decision.

We live in an age dominated by economics, in which many people assume that we are all rational, self-interested actors who would never do anything for anyone else unless we were confident that we would receive an equal or greater return. Yet the economic value of the goods and services that we bestow on one another as gifts vastly exceeds the value of what we exchange through transactions. Just consider the value of all the work people perform without monetary compensation to raise a family. In the vast majority of cases, such unpaid laborers could not earn enough money to replace themselves. More importantly, they wouldn't want to.

Some people are tempted to dismiss those who opt to care for their families as sentimental or weak-willed, either unable or unwilling to enter the rough-and-tumble world of the marketplace and make the most of their earning power. Others might even accuse such people of failing to pull their own weight and thereby exerting a drag on the economy.

In fact, however, earning money is not the sole basis for human existence, and it would be a mistake to suppose that human beings who earn larger sums of money are leading more worthwhile or better lives than those who earn less. Many admirable people choose to pursue sufficient wealth to be able to serve rather than shed their service commitments to earn more money.

Many of the things in life we cherish most are not susceptible to economic valuation. What is the value of a hug, of a heart-to-heart conversation, of knowing there is someone in the world you can always count on and truly be yourself with? To ask what a good wife or husband, a good son or daughter, a good mother or father is worth is to seriously misunderstand what it means to be part of such a relationship. The question of monetary valuation never enters the picture, because it is inherently out of place and necessarily degrades that which it seeks to appraise. We are worth a great deal more to one another than we can describe or explain in economic terms.

The Bible is often regarded as a supremely patriarchal work in which most women are relegated to minor and subservient roles. Nonetheless, some female figures in the Bible play roles every bit as important—and sometimes even more important—than those played by men. One particularly shining example of feminine leadership is found in the in the book of Genesis story of Rebecca.

Although as a woman Rebecca does not wield the same rights to property and authority as the men in her life, she manages to do more than any of them to ensure the fulfillment of a higher purpose. Her story illuminates family life as an opportunity for service. For believers and nonbelievers alike, Rebecca's story shows how a person lacking conventional means of wealth, power, and prestige can still exert a profound influence over the course of events, enabling others to know themselves and become who they are meant to be.

Rebecca does not do what her family members think they want, nor does she shy away from challenging them in ways they find threatening. Yet in the end, her service brings everyone to life.

The name "Rebecca" comes from a Semitic root meaning to tie together, join, or secure. In view of Rebecca's roles in the biblical narrative—daughter-in-law of Abraham and Sarah, wife of Isaac, mother of Esau and Jacob, and grandmother of Joseph and his brothers—the name seems entirely appropriate.

Rebecca is called on to play vital roles. For one thing, she literally gives birth to the next generation of patriarchs. Even more importantly, she transmits the covenantal torch from the generation of Abraham to the generation of Jacob, a charge that her husband, Isaac, proves himself rather ill-equipped to carry out. Without Rebecca, an essential link in the chain spanning generations would have been missing.

The book of Genesis tells us that when Abraham was a very old man and still had no children, God made a covenant with him, saying that Abraham would have many, many descendants. This declaration was so preposterous that Abraham fell on his face and laughed, knowing that it was impossible for such an old man and his old wife, Sarah, to have children.

Yet the story tells us that God did not waver in his assurance that Abraham would have a son, Isaac ("he laughed"), through whom the covenant would pass. Isaac is born, and because he will need a wife to fulfill this destiny, the birth of Rebecca is foretold, albeit anonymously, soon thereafter. Some years later, Isaac now grown into an adult, his father receives divine instructions to take his son to a mountain to offer him as a sacrifice. At the last moment, the order is belayed, and Isaac's life is spared.

We can only speculate about the damage such an experience must have done to Isaac, but when the time arrives for him to marry, his father sends not his son but a servant to select a bride. The servant decides he will devise a test to determine whether he has found the right woman: He will go to a well and ask for water. If the woman at the well offers to draw water not only for him, but also for his ten camels, he will know she is the one.

To his surprise, the first woman he approaches does exactly that—a considerable task, in view of the large quantities of water a camel can drink. This generous young woman, who agrees to leave with the servant to meet her betrothed the very next day, is Rebecca.

As Rebecca's entourage approaches the home of Abraham, they see Isaac out in the fields. But Isaac does not see them, perhaps an indication that he is not as far-sighted as his bride-to-be. Isaac then brings her into his mother's tent and loves her.

As had been the case for Abraham and Sarah, Isaac and Rebecca are childless, and it appears again that the covenantal chain will be broken. But Isaac prays, and eventually Rebecca conceives. Her pregnancy is a difficult one, and she prays for understanding. God speaks to her, telling her that she is bearing twins who will be in conflict with each other. The first to be born is Esau, followed by Jacob. As the boys grow, Esau becomes a man's man, a skillful hunter and man of the open country, while Jacob is content to stay at home among the tents.

One day Esau returns from the hunt complaining that he is famished. He asks his brother for a bowl of soup. Jacob replies that to satisfy his hunger, Esau must first sell his birthright, the elder son's claim as the firstborn to the property of their father. Esau, protesting that the birthright will be of no use if he starves to death, complies. He is the sort of man who gives in to the urges of his belly, preferring a bowl of soup today to a birthright that will not be redeemable for many years.

Esau's conduct raises serious questions about his fitness to receive the inheritance that Abraham passed to his son Isaac. He prefers the life of sensation, hunting and fishing, to the interpersonal relationships that form the basis of domestic life. As we will see, when he is thwarted, his first impulse is to respond with force, not cunning and calculation. He literally despises his birthright for a mess of pottage. Perhaps he lacks the larger vision and capacity to delay gratification that the bearer of the birthright will need.

Jacob, on the other hand, though certainly no moral exemplar, shows himself capable of adopting the long view. He is prepared to take short-term risks in pursuit of larger gains. He does not blithely toss things away, but seeks to profit from what he has, even when dealing with his own brother.

When two people compete, it is natural to assume that the spoils will go to the stronger, but the competition between Esau and Jacob shows that the stronger does not always prevail. Instead, the brother who sees the bigger picture rises to the challenge. Perhaps for these reasons, Isaac loves Esau, but Rebecca loves Jacob.

When Esau is forty years old, the same age at which his father married, he takes as wives two Hittite women, who are a source of grief to Isaac and Rebecca. This is perhaps because Isaac and Rebecca recognize that any children of these women would likely be raised according to Hittite traditions, worshipping other gods rather than the God of Abraham and Isaac. If God's covenant with Abraham is to be passed down through the next generation, it will require the cooperation—perhaps even the enthusiasm—of one of their sons' wives. Once again, Esau has chosen in a way that does not put the covenant first.

With these events as prologue, the story now moves to the disposition of the covenantal blessing, which declares that its bearer's descendants will be "as numerous as the stars of the sky . . . and through these offspring all nations on earth will be blessed." In other words, the covenant is a blessing to *a particular people*, but through it, *all people* are meant to benefit. Hence the manner in which the covenant passes to the next generation is of concern not just to the family of Abraham, but to all humankind, for the welfare of humanity writ large hangs in the balance. There is a great deal riding on the shoulders of the person to whom the covenant passes.

We are told that Isaac, whose vision has never been particularly strong, has now grown old and can no longer see. He calls Esau and tells him that, suspecting that his own end is near, he wants Esau to go out into the field to hunt wild game and prepare for him his favorite dish so that he can give Esau his blessing before he dies. Here we see why Isaac might prefer Esau to Jacob—because Isaac too is a man of limited vision who thinks more with his belly than his head. He is not interested in proof that his son can see the big picture and subordinate short-term inconveniences to long-term victory. Instead, he is thinking about his next meal.

If the covenant is to be protected and served by its next bearer, the guidance of a more perspicacious steward is going to be needed. And this is precisely what Rebecca proves herself to be. Hearing Isaac speak to Esau, she calls Jacob and tells him to listen carefully to her: "Go out to the flock and bring me two choice goats, so that I can prepare tasty food for your father. Then take it to your father to eat, so that he may give you his blessing before he dies." Rebecca knows that neither of her sons is perfect, but she knows better than Isaac which is the most fit to bear the covenantal blessing, and she calls Jacob to act as an accomplice in directing it his way.

Jacob's response is also revealing: "But Esau is a hairy man. If my father touches me I would appear to be tricking him and would bring down a curse rather than a blessing." As usual, Jacob the schemer is thinking things through, anticipating every eventuality, and he quite reasonably fears that his mother's scheme could go disastrously awry.

It is Rebecca who acts fearlessly at this point, telling Jacob, "Let the curse fall on me." So important is the covenant that Rebecca will brave even her husband's curse rather than let it fall into the wrong hands. More than any other character in the story, Rebecca is the one who acts courageously.

So Jacob does as his mother bids him, bringing her the goats, and she prepares the tasty food. She takes Esau's clothes and puts them on Jacob and covers his hands and neck with the goatskins, so that should his father touch him, he will feel rough and hairy like Esau. Jacob then goes to his father, and when Isaac asks who he is, he replies: "I am Esau, your firstborn son. I have done as you told me. Please sit up and eat some of my game, so that you may give me your blessing." Isaac expresses amazement that he found the game so quickly, but Jacob explains that "the Lord your God gave me success." Still not convinced, Isaac asks him to come near so that he can touch him and know whether he is indeed Esau.

Isaac says, "The voice is the voice of Jacob, but the hands are the hands of Esau." He then proceeds to bless Jacob, but then he pauses again and asks, "Are you really my son Esau?" To which Jacob responds, "I am." Isaac then asks for some of the game, so he can eat it. After he eats, he again calls Jacob close, and when he catches the smell of his clothes, he bestows the blessing upon him: "The smell of my son is like the smell of the field the Lord has blessed. May God give you heaven's dew and earth's richness."

No sooner has Isaac finished his blessing and Jacob left his father's presence than Esau comes in from hunting. He urges his father to sit up and eat some of his game so that Jacob might give him his blessing. "Who are you?" Isaac asks incredulously. "I am your son, your firstborn, Esau," he answers. At these words, Isaac "trembles violently." We do not know for sure why Isaac trembles. It could be that he is simply enraged. But there is another possibility: He senses that something beyond his ken, let alone his control, has acted through him, in relation to which he serves as a mere conduit.

Isaac tells his son that someone else just brought him game, and that person received the blessing. Esau begs his father, "Bless me too, my father." But Isaac tells him that his brother came deceitfully and took his blessing. Esau responds that Jacob is named rightly—the supplanter. "Haven't you reserved any blessing for me?" he pleads. Isaac tells Esau that he has made his brother lord over him. Again, Esau begs, "Have you only one blessing? Bless me, too, father." Finally Isaac does bless Esau, but it is not the covenantal blessing. Full of anger, Esau resolves that once the days of mourning for his father are over, he will kill his brother.

When Rebecca hears what Esau has said, she warns Jacob that his brother is planning to avenge himself. She urges Jacob to flee to her brother's house and stay with him while Esau's anger subsides. She tells him that once Esau has forgotten, she will send word for the younger brother to return. Otherwise, she says, she would lose them both in a day.

Next Rebecca turns to her husband and says that she is disgusted with the Hittite women. If Jacob follows Esau in taking one for his wife, she warns, her life will not be worth living. In terms of her role as steward of the covenant, this may be quite true, since it is vital that Jacob's wife raise their children in the faith of Abraham and Isaac.

Isaac calls for Jacob and blesses him. Then he tells him to go to his maternal grandfather's house and there to take one of his uncle's daughters as his wife. After saying so, he bestows on Jacob the true covenantal blessing: "May God bless you and make you fruitful and increase your numbers until you become a community of peoples. May he give you and your descendants the blessing given to Abraham."

Hearing that Isaac commanded Jacob not to marry a Canaanite woman, Esau goes and marries one of his uncle's daughters, in addition to the wives he already has.

Though Rebecca promised to send for Jacob, she never does so, and so she never sees her son again. She dies before the brothers are reconciled.

Some regard Rebecca's conduct in this story as reprehensible. After all, she appears to be guilty of a number of serious breaches. First, she arranges to deprive her firstborn son of his blessing. Second, she deceives her husband and subverts his will, replacing Esau with Jacob. And third, she engages Jacob as a co-conspirator in this web of deception. Even when the subterfuge has been completed, she continues along the same path, seizing as a pretext for Jacob's departure the fear that he will marry a woman who worships other gods. This cements her reputation as a master manipulator. She wants Jacob to leave so that he may live, but she is also genuinely fearful that he might marry the wrong woman.

Yet there are many reasons to think highly of Rebecca. Her conduct at the well toward Abraham's servant establishes her generosity. She clearly hears her calling and is prepared to leave her family right away. This call will require her to marry a man whose father does not trust him to choose whom to marry, a choice that is accorded to her. Like her mother-in-law, she has trouble conceiving, and her pregnancy is a difficult one. She inquires of God, who speaks directly to her, telling her that her two sons will be at odds and that the older will serve the younger, information she does not share with her husband. This suggests that Rebecca's preference for Jacob is divinely ordained.

Unlike Isaac, Rebecca is able to step outside of her own culture and tradition, especially as it concerns primogeniture, the rights of the firstborn. More important to both God and Rebecca than birth order are the talents and characters of her offspring, which do not always favor the eldest. Rebecca knows her sons better than their father, and she does what she can within the constraints under which she operates to ensure that the covenant passes to the divinely ordained son, the crafty one who sees the bigger picture and is able to hold his impulses in check. Isaac loves food, but Rebecca loves something far more enduring.

From Rebecca's point of view, the deception of Isaac may in fact represent something radically different—the opening of Isaac's eyes. Rebecca cannot force her husband to bestow the blessing on Jacob. Nor, perhaps, can she persuade him by argument. Instead, she puts Jacob in the position of the firstborn and enables Isaac to "see for himself" how much better the role fits Jacob than Esau. After the deception is complete and Esau asks for a blessing, Isaac extends one to him, but it is not the covenantal blessing. Only afterward does he bestow the covenantal blessing on Jacob. He trembles because, thanks to Rebecca, he finally sees what he never saw before—that Jacob is the one.

Rebecca serves her family: Isaac, who cannot see which of his sons is better suited to bear the covenant; Esau, who lacks the imagination and character to fulfill the responsibility of a covenant bearer; Jacob, who lacks the insight and courage to secure the covenant for himself. She also serves Abraham's many descendants, whose future lives depend on a successful covenantal transfer, and even God, as she bound herself to God's vision that the older would serve the younger. If necessary, she is prepared to risk everything, even to be cursed by her own husband, rather than let his weakness thwart the will of God. In short, she is wise, steadfast, and courageous.

In an age when we sometimes prize autonomy before everything else, it can be difficult to admit that we often want things that are not in anyone's best interest. Rebecca knows that if Isaac could see clearly his sons' natures in the context of what is truly at stake, he would think less of his own belly and more about future bearers of the Abrahamic covenant. True, she subverts his will by replacing the elder with the younger, but she does so in a way that enables Isaac to see for himself, and when he does see, he recognizes that Jacob is the more fitting recipient of the blessing. He still could give it to Esau, but he doesn't.

Every family, community, and society needs people who can see beyond the pressing concerns of the moment and focus on broader and longer-term responsibilities. It takes less vision to go through life lurching from one crisis to the next, but only those who see beyond today and have their eyes fixed on a more distant target can hope to move a group of people in a truly good direction. This is precisely what Rebecca is able to do. She is a steward not only of her family, but of all humankind, acting on behalf of what Isaac should choose until he is able to do so for himself.

This service brings Rebecca's family to life. She is not numbered among the patriarchs, but her excellence as matriarch propels the covenantal blessing along the appropriate path in a way that leaves everyone standing. The first fraternal confrontation in the book of Genesis ended in fratricide, when a jealous Cain killed his brother Abel. Thanks to Rebecca, a recurrence of the primeval fratricide is averted. Isaac, who thought himself on the point of death, ends up living a good many more years, and Esau and Jacob are eventually reconciled. Rebecca dies before she can secure or witness this reconciliation, but she has set them all on a path that makes it possible.

Just as Rebecca's birth was foretold to Abraham, so her influence continues past her death. This is a sure sign of a person who has come fully to life—that they live in connection with purposes that were active before their birth and that persist long after they are gone. When the occasion demands, Rebecca plays the role of steward better than anyone in her generation. She loves her husband and sons not only for who they are, but for who they are capable of becoming. In treating them in some ways as though each had already become that person, she draws them farther along on the path of their development.

Rebecca exemplifies one of the greatest possible forms of service. She acts with a clear vision not only of what the family is, but of what it is called to be. She is focused not just on meeting immediate needs, but on a larger, longer-term destiny. Instead of confirming the prejudices of her husband and sons, she challenges them to become better than they are by serving purposes larger than themselves.

In this sense, Rebecca is implicitly inviting them to emulate her own conduct by recognizing these larger purposes for which they are prepared to lay down their lives. She leads them beyond the cramped confines of their own security and comfort, enabling them to come more fully to life by becoming something more than they are.

five

BENJAMIN
Service to Community

IN HIS 2000 BOOK, *BOWLING ALONE: THE COLLAPSE AND REVIVAL OF AMERICAN Community*, Robert D. Putnam describes a precipitous erosion in civic engagement in the United States. He details the disintegration of a Pennsylvania bridge club, the withering away of a Virginia chapter of the NAACP, the collapse of an Illinois Veterans of Foreign Wars post, and the sinking into senescence of the Charity League of Dallas. The problem, Putnam argues, is that the senior members dropping out of such organizations are not being renewed by fresh recruits.

To Putnam, this decline is particularly perplexing in light of the fact that in the 1960s participation in community organizations appeared to be increasing. Americans had more leisure time on their hands than ever before and thus more time to give to service activities. Their challenge was less to find more time for work than to determine how to make good use of their time when work was done.

The book's title, *Bowling Alone*, reflects the fact that although the number of people who bowl had increased over the past several decades, the number of people who bowl in leagues had declined. When people bowl alone—just as when they go to the movies, watch TV, surf the internet, and even attend worship services alone—they opt not to participate in the kinds of social interactions and civic discussions on which a thriving democracy depends.

Critics have argued that Putnam's thesis is flawed—that, for example, such declines in civic life were under way long before the period he examines and that in fact old kinds of social ties were being replaced with new ones. Whether Putnam's diagnosis of a decline in American civic life is on target or not, the important discussion into which he draws us raises the question, Are we becoming more or less tightly bound to one another in community?

A lot is at stake in this question, in part because some of our most important opportunities to come to life are associated with shared activities, interests, and commitments. Examples include worship services, youth sports and scouting activities, and book clubs. When we are alone, we are not building community, and a decline in community service deprives us of many opportunities to come more fully to life.

When it comes to understanding the difference a single person can make in a community, perhaps the greatest example in the history of the United States is Benjamin Franklin (1706–1790). Known today for his incredibly wide range of contributions to literature, science, and statesmanship, Franklin was, from a very early age, perhaps the most active and influential figure ever to stride the streets of Philadelphia. Born in Boston, Franklin came to his adopted city a fugitive, having fled an apprenticeship in the Boston printing shop of his brother James.

The city Franklin would make his home was a far cry from the sprawling metropolis we know today as Philadelphia. Founded in 1682 by William Penn, by 1720 it had grown to a population of ten thousand. Like most large American cities at the time, its roads were unpaved and could become impassable with heavy rains. The streets were often strewn with garbage, animals ran about, and the quality of life, by material standards, was not high. Enter Franklin, a genius who seemed to view every apparently intractable civic problem as an opportunity for practical innovation and social collaboration.

Franklin is the American philanthropist par excellence. Although the amount of money he donated pales in comparison to that bestowed by a Carnegie, a Rockefeller, or Bill Gates, he did more—far more—than just give away money. Many of his collaborative ventures resulted in customs, inventions, and institutions that continue to thrive today, not only in Philadelphia and the United States but around the world. Though Franklin earned and gave away a fortune, he also chose to forego many opportunities to profit from his works.

What made Benjamin Franklin tick? Part of the answer, of course, was the sheer genius of this polymath, who was a writer, inventor, scientist, musician, politician, and philanthropist—among many other labels one might use to characterize the breadth of his abilities and interests. But Franklin was far more than merely clever. He seems to have looked at other people, his community, and all people from a particularly fruitful point of view. He was an extraordinarily curious person, on the lookout almost all the time for new opportunities to learn. He was willing to engage in conversation with just about anyone, regardless of their wealth or social station. And he seems to have harbored a huge ambition to make a difference, leaving people and places better off than they had been when he arrived.

Consider one of Franklin's lesser-known achievements—charting the North Atlantic Gulf Stream. Each time Franklin sailed back and forth between North America and Europe, he avoided whiling away the days in idle pursuits. Instead, he kept his eyes and his inquiring mind open. He noticed that a vessel could travel eastward across the Atlantic in half the time required for the westward journey. He sought an explanation from sailors and eventually determined that the Atlantic Ocean harbored an eastward-flowing "river in the ocean," which could be exploited to speed mail delivery and commercial shipping.

Contributions

Benjamin Franklin was an extraordinary human being many times over. Any number of his interests and pursuits taken alone would be sufficient to establish him as an important figure in history, even had all of his achievements been confined to one sphere of endeavor. Consider this partial list of his contributions:

Printer—As a teenager, Franklin began his multifaceted career as an apprentice in his brother's printing shop. However, he was stung by his brother's lack of appreciation, so he set off on his own, eventually establishing himself as one of America's first "media moguls," building a chain of franchised printing shops and newspapers in the colonies. Despite his commercial success, Franklin saw printing as far more than a means of making money. He regarded it as a means of instructing his fellow citizens in the moral virtues necessary to build and sustain good communities.

Publisher—Franklin's *Poor Richard's Almanack*, for which he wrote much of the copy and which was published annually from 1732 to 1758, soon established itself as one of the most popular publications in the colonies, the number-one best seller of its day. Franklin wrote under a pseudonym, but everyone soon knew who was behind it. Before long, many of his adages, such as "Early to bed and early to rise, makes a man healthy, wealthy, and wise," and "Three may keep a secret, if two of them are dead," became permanent fixtures of American conversation.

Writer—Franklin began writing pseudonymously as a teenager in his brother's print shop as "Silence Dogood." Over the course of his life he developed into one of the most widely known and influential authors in US history. His autobiography, on which he labored at various points during his life but which was published only after his death, has become a classic of the genre. It is still studied today for its portraits of early American history, its literary merit, and its usefulness as a guide to self-improvement.

Scientist—Franklin made numerous scientific contributions, the best known of which concerned electricity. He developed the concepts of positive and negative charge and established the principle of the conservation of charge. He developed a famous experiment with a kite (which he may have never conducted) to prove that lightning is an electrical phenomenon. He was elected a fellow of the Royal Society, receiving its Copley Medal—the equivalent of today's Nobel Prize—and ranked as one of the two or three most famous scientists in the world during his lifetime.

Inventor—Franklin is credited with a wide range of important inventions, including the lightning rod, bifocal eyeglasses, the flexible urinary catheter, and the Franklin stove. The stove produced more heat with less fuel and generated less smoke than other fireplaces of his day. Franklin, a rich man from his publishing endeavors, never patented any of his inventions, explaining, "As we enjoy great advantages from the inventions of others, we should be glad of an opportunity to serve others by any invention of ours."

Statesman—Franklin's political contributions are well known, but one way to appreciate their singular significance is to note that Franklin was the only person to sign the Declaration of Independence, the Treaty of Alliance with France (which made it possible for the United States to triumph in the revolutionary war against Britain), the Treaty of Paris (which concluded the war on favorable terms for the United States), and the US Constitution. In each case, Franklin not only signed the document but played a central role in creating it.

Social innovator—Franklin founded or cofounded a number of important civic organizations, including one of the first volunteer fire departments, the colonies' first lending library, the first hospital in the colonies, the first secular university in the United States (now known as the University of Pennsylvania), and the American Philosophical Society, to help scientists share their investigations, theories, and discoveries. Franklin was also one of his day's most ardent proponents of the abolition of slavery, the topic of his last published work.

Moralist—Franklin recognized that the United States could survive only if its citizens were virtuous, creating an educational challenge that the state could never meet without hazarding tyranny. Though for much of his life he was not Christian in the conventional sense, Franklin believed that morality has a divine basis and saw the hand of divine providence at work in the struggle for US independence. He also famously argued for daily prayer at the Constitutional Convention and designed a version of the Great Seal of the United States that featured the Israelites crossing the divided Red Sea with the Egyptians in hot pursuit. His proposed motto for the new nation: Rebellion to Tyrants Is Obedience to God.

Polymath—This brief account leaves out more of Franklin's achievements than it mentions, including his important contributions as a freemason, political theorist, postmaster, diplomat, and revolutionary. Franklin also did as much as anyone to build the mythology of the founding of the United States. Looking at the back of President George Washington's chair at the Constitutional Convention, for example, Franklin said he often wondered whether the sun on it was on its way up or down. After the convention concluded successfully, he remarked, "I have the happiness to know that it is a rising and not a setting sun."

Of course, Franklin was no saint. He never married his common-law wife, Deborah Read. The two raised his illegitimate son, William, whose mother remains a mystery to this day. Their biological son, Francis, died of smallpox after Franklin chose not to have him inoculated, a decision he regretted his whole life. Franklin eventually broke with and disowned William over the latter's Loyalist position. In 1745, Franklin penned a letter titled "Advice to a Young Man on the Choice of a Mistress," the title of which speaks for itself.

Even some of Franklin's most illustrious contemporaries harbored reservations about the great man's legacy. For example, John Adams worried that Franklin's role in the founding would in years to come become so magnified that it would overshadow other important contributors, including Adams himself. In 1790 he wrote to a friend: "The History of our Revolution will be one continued Lye [*sic*] from one End to the other. The Essence of the whole will be *that Dr Franklins electrical Rod, Smote the Earth and out Spring [sic] General Washington. That Franklin electrified him with his Rod—and thence forward these two conducted all the Policy Negotiations Legislation and War."*

Life

To understand how Franklin managed to contribute so much to his community and to community building more generally, it is important to know more about his life. And the story of Franklin's life is nearly as remarkable as his extraordinary range of achievements.

Franklin was born in Boston in 1706, the last son of seventeen children of Josiah Franklin, a candle maker (he had seven children with his first wife, Anne, and ten more with his second wife, Abiah). Franklin's father intended him to become a clergyman, but finances prevented Ben from receiving more than two years of formal schooling, which ended when he was ten years old. Despite his meager formal education, a deep love of learning was central to Ben's life from an early age, and he later wrote, "From a child I was fond of reading, and all the little money that came into my hands was ever laid out in books."

After working for his father, Ben was apprenticed to his brother, James, a printer, when he was twelve years old. Soon after Ben turned fifteen, his brother founded the first truly independent newspaper in the colonies. Through him Ben learned the trade of printing, which would provide him a lifelong means of supporting himself and disseminating his ideas. Yet James was also a harsh disciplinarian, and Ben came to regard his apprenticeship as his first encounter with tyranny. Soon it also provided the occasion for his first experiences of rebellion and liberation.

When James refused to print his brother's letters in the paper, Ben began surreptitiously submitting his pieces under the pseudonym Silence Dogood. The Dogood letters quickly became quite popular, and after they ceased, James pleaded in print with their unknown author to make his or her identity known. When James learned that young Ben was responsible for them, he was not pleased.

When Franklin was seventeen, he abandoned his apprenticeship and sailed to Philadelphia. After finding work in printing shops, he was persuaded by the state's governor to travel to London. There he spent two years, again working as a printer.

Upon Franklin's return to Philadelphia, he worked in several printing shops before finding a partner and setting up his own. A year later, in 1729, he began publishing the *Pennsylvania Gazette*, which served as an outlet for his prodigious creativity, including the invention of a number of fictitious characters who served as his mouthpieces. He saw the paper, as he would later see his almanac, as a means of elevating the intellectual and moral sensibilities of his fellow colonists. He also entered into a common-law marriage with Deborah Read, to whom he had been linked as a teenager, after her first husband abandoned her.

Advancements in Franklin's life came frequently. When he was twenty-four he began publishing *Poor Richard's Almanack*. In that same year he was selected to be the official printer of Pennsylvania. Soon thereafter he joined the Freemasons, quickly rising to become Grand Master of the Pennsylvania lodge, which helped to propel him along in his business and political careers. In 1737, he was appointed Postmaster of Philadelphia. In 1741 he began advertising his Franklin stove, and in 1743 he laid the groundwork for the American Philosophical Society. By 1746 he was conducting experiments with electricity. In 1753 he received honorary degrees from Harvard and Yale.

In 1757 he embarked on a long career of intermittent foreign service, first as an agent for several of the colonies. In 1774, after forty-four years of marriage, Deborah died. The next year Franklin was elected to the Continental Congress and as Postmaster General of the colonies. In 1776, he presided over Pennsylvania's Constitutional Convention, served on a committee that drafted the Declaration of Independence, and arrived in Paris to represent the colonies in their quest for freedom from British rule.

In 1778 he signed the French Alliance, and then in 1779 he was appointed to negotiate peace with England. After signing the peace treaty, he invented bifocals, secured election as the president of the Pennsylvania Executive Council (equivalent to the governorship), and in 1787 signed the US Constitution. In 1789 he became president of the Pennsylvania Abolition Society. In 1790 at the age of eighty-four, he died. At least twenty thousand mourners attended his funeral. He was buried in Christ Church Burial Ground in Philadelphia.

The range and magnitude of Franklin's contributions are unparalleled, and it is no accident that he is often referred to as the "greatest American." Washington may have been more indispensable, Lincoln may have captured the spirit of the nation more eloquently, and Jefferson may have risen to higher office, but Franklin has no equal for the sheer range and magnitude of his contributions. During his lifetime, he was one of the best-known and most-admired people in the world.

The Junto

Among Franklin's most innovative contributions is one that is both unknown to most Americans and serves as one of the best illustrations of how serving the community can bring a person to life. When Franklin was only twenty-one years old, he founded an organization he called the Junto, borrowing a term for political groups that was in fairly wide use in Britain during the eighteenth century. Franklin, who had only two years of formal schooling, sought even at this young age to create a school of citizenry among his neighbors and fellow businessmen.

Also known as the Leather Apron Club, it would consist, in Franklin's words, of "a group of like-minded aspiring artisans and tradesmen who hoped to improve themselves while they improved their community." Drawing on the model of English coffeehouses, which Franklin knew well from the years he had spent in

London, he saw the Junto as a means of fostering discussion around ethical, political, and scientific ideas and sharing business experiences.

The group initially consisted of twelve members, drawing from Franklin's circle of friends and fellow entrepreneurs in Philadelphia. Among the walks of life represented were printer, surveyor, cabinetmaker, clerk, cobbler, gentleman, and tavern owner. Although Franklin was the youngest of the group, he was also its acknowledged prime mover. The Junto met weekly on Friday evenings at a local tavern, where the order of business, as described by Franklin, was the following:

> The rules that I drew up required that every member, in his turn, should produce one or more queries on any point of morals, politics, or natural philosophy to be discussed by the company, and once in three months produce and read an essay of his own writing, on any subject he pleased. Our debates were to be under the direction of a president, and to be conducted in the sincere spirit of inquiry after truth, without fondness for dispute or desire of victory, and to prevent warmth, all expressions of positiveness in opinions, or direct contradiction, were after some time made contraband, and prohibited under small pecuniary penalties.

Franklin devised a list of questions to be used as a point of departure for conversation, with the intention that good ideas would find expression in practical works for the benefit of the community. The discussions they helped to spawn led to social innovations such as the volunteer fire brigade and the colonies' first hospital. Among these questions were:

- "Have you met with any thing in the author you last read, remarkable, or suitable for communication to the Junto? particularly in history, morality, poetry, physics, travels, mechanic arts, or other parts of knowledge?"
- "What new story have you lately heard agreeable for telling in conversation?"
- "Hath any citizen in your knowledge failed in his business lately, and what have you heard of the cause?"
- "Have you lately heard of any citizen's thriving well, and by what means?"
- "Have you lately heard how any present rich man, here or elsewhere, got his estate?"
- "Do you know of any fellow citizen, who has lately done a worthy action, deserving praise and imitation? or who has committed an error proper for us to be warned against and avoid?"
- "Have you lately observed any encroachment on the just liberties of the people?"
- "Have you any weighty affair in hand, in which you think the advice of the Junto may be of service?"
- "Do you see any thing amiss in the present customs or proceedings of the Junto, which might be amended?"

This list of questions is notable for many reasons, but perhaps most remarkable is its multiple spheres of concern. First, members are interested in improving their own lives and the lives of their colleagues. Second, they seek to improve the lives of people in their community. Third, they see the Junto as a society of mutual aid, in which each member will come to both the material and moral support of the others. Finally, the members are committed to improving the Junto itself, by thinking self-critically and constructively about its work.

The procedure for admitting new members carries this spirit even further. Upon gaining admittance, a new member was to stand, place his hand over his heart, and respond to the following questions:

- "Have you any particular disrespect to any present members? *Answer.* I have not."
- "Do you sincerely declare that you love mankind in general; of what profession or religion soever? *Answ.* I do."
- "Do you think any person ought to be harmed in his body, name or goods, for mere speculative opinions, or his external way of worship? *Answ.* No."
- "Do you love truth for truth's sake, and will you endeavor impartially to find and receive it yourself and communicate it to others? *Answ.* Yes."

As this custom makes clear, the Junto was to be an organization in which members sought to learn from and help one another, scrupulously avoiding causes for dissension and strife. Potentially divisive matters such as personality, social identity, and religious affiliation were meant to give way to a shared pursuit of truth and flourishing. It did not matter what people espoused as long as they did not allow their beliefs to get in the way of the pursuit of mutual enlightenment, replacing the tendency to build barriers between people with a commitment to forge collaboration and fellowship.

The Junto represented a practical expression of Franklin's vision of the purposes to which he felt called in life—a vision that runs counter to many of the most pervasive features of popular culture today. Though he was one of the wealthiest, most powerful, and most famous people of his day, he did not see wealth, power, or fame as ends in themselves. When at age forty-three Franklin chose to step away from business, he did so recognizing that a life of accumulation cannot measure up to a life of service to the community.

Although Franklin undoubtedly took great pleasure in his commercial success, his influence over practical affairs, and his world-wide renown, his greatest happiness lay in service. He genuinely hoped to improve the lot of his fellow human beings, as reflected in the founding of the first hospital, volunteer fire department, and lending library, as well as the American Philosophical Society and innumerable civic projects, such as paving and lighting Philadelphia's streets. The Junto served as a generator of practical ideas for enhancing community life.

Franklin sought not only to serve, but also to engage others in service, drawing people together around a shared vision of a flourishing community. Here lies one of the marks of a truly great philanthropist—to help others, but in ways that help them become helpers themselves. Franklin's philanthropy promoted self-sufficiency in the economic and political spheres. It also fostered a sense of mutual responsibility and helped others experience the fulfillment that comes from working together for the common good.

In fact, Franklin anticipated the writings of a number of other later philanthropists—perhaps most notably Andrew Carnegie in an article called "The Gospel of Wealth"—in warning against the dangers of the kind of giving that leads to dependence. Concerning the effort to improve the lot of the poor, Franklin wrote:

> I am for doing good to the poor, but I differ in opinion of the means. I think the best way of doing good to the poor, is not making them easy *in* poverty, but leading or driving them *out* of it. In my youth I travelled much, and I observed in different countries, that the more public provisions were made for the poor, the less they provided for themselves, and of course became poorer. And, on the contrary, the less was done for them, the more they did for themselves, and became richer.

Of course, Franklin recognized that some people lacked the means—bodily or mental—to provide for themselves. But where the capacity for self-sufficiency was present, he found that challenging people to develop self-sufficiency was the most philanthropically appropriate course of action.

As a great innovator, Franklin savored a certain degree of uncertainty, and he regarded a readiness to take risks as an essential feature of a thriving community. To fail to attempt anything genuinely new, which always entails some degree of risk, is to forego the opportunity of improvement. He saw this principle as applying in all realms of human life, from the scientific to the political.

To call the system of government he helped to fashion an experiment was second nature to Franklin, and he urged his fellow citizens to take substantial risks for the sake of great rewards: "Those who would give up essential liberty, to purchase a little temporary safety, deserve neither liberty nor safety." With every generation, Franklin knew, freedom requires a new crop of zealous guardians and defenders.

The French political philosopher Alexis de Tocqueville, author of *Democracy in America* (1835–1840) and one of the greatest students of America who ever lived, marveled at the extraordinary capacity of Americans to join together through voluntary associations. He regarded this as the core of American genius, reflecting the legacy of Benjamin Franklin more than that of any other individual. For a democracy to thrive, it needs civic-minded citizens, and the voluntary association is the most important school of citizenship.

Franklin's newspapers, the almanac, and his tracts and treatises were all aimed at helping Americans become better educated, more engaged, and more responsible citizens and human beings. In 1737 Franklin printed an essay, "On Freedom of Speech and the Press," that stated: "Freedom of speech is a principal pillar of a free government; when this support is taken away, the constitution of a free society is dissolved, and tyranny is erected on its ruins. Republics and limited monarchies derive their strength and vigor from a popular examination into the action of the magistrates." He sought not only to protect free speech but to give people a clear sense of what it could amount to, thereby promoting literacy, education, and engagement in civic affairs.

Franklin envisioned a nation whose strength would lie less in the capacity of its army and navy to wage war than in the vitality and civic virtue of its citizenry. When writing in 1749 on the aims of educating young people, he said: "When they [Youth] ardently desire of Victory, for the Sake of the Praise attending it, they will begin to feel the Want, and be sensible of the Use of *Logic*, or the Art of Reasoning to *discover* Truth, and of Arguing to *defend* it, and *convince* Adversaries." Military power may be able to produce temporary victories, but nations endure for generations only if they remain true and just and persuade others to do the same.

So committed was Franklin to the cultivation of civic virtue that he even composed his own list of thirteen virtues, which are enumerated in his autobiography, one of the nation's first and most successful self-help books:

1. Temperance: Eat not to dullness. Drink not to elevation.
2. Silence: Speak not but what may benefit others or yourself. Avoid trifling conversation.
3. Order: Let all your things have their places. Let each part of your business have its time.
4. Resolution: Resolve to perform what you ought. Perform without fail what you resolve.
5. Frugality: Make no expense but to do good to others or yourself: i.e., Waste nothing.
6. Industry: Lose no time. Be always employed in something useful. Cut off all unnecessary actions.
7. Sincerity: Use no hurtful deceit. Think innocently and justly; and if you speak, speak accordingly.
8. Justice: Wrong none by doing injuries, or omitting the benefits that are your duty.
9. Moderation: Avoid extremes. Forbear resenting injuries so much as you think they deserve.
10. Cleanliness: Tolerate no uncleanliness in body, clothes, or habitation.
11. Tranquility: Be not disturbed at trifles, or at accidents common or unavoidable.
12. Chastity: Rarely use venery but for health or offspring; never to dullness, weakness, or the injury of your own or another's peace or reputation.
13. Humility: Imitate Jesus and Socrates.

Franklin attributed his own success in large part to his sustained attention to these excellences, and he encouraged his readers to do the same. Constitutions and bills of rights had a vital role to play, but they could not long secure a republic unless the citizens themselves were virtuous.

Franklin, himself the product of no aristocracy, saw in ordinary people the potential for greatness, the capacity to make signal contributions in every field of endeavor. What was needed was not a system of hereditary entitlement, but opportunities for people to learn and challenges to do better. Again, Franklin embodied one of the core attributes of the great philanthropist—the belief that people are capable of more than they know.

Franklin's faith in the capacity of ordinary people extended to one quite extraordinary group: slaves. His conviction that slavery was unjust was grounded in part in empirical observations. He had visited a "Negro School" and wrote in 1763 that "I was on the whole much pleas'd, and from what I then saw, have conceiv'd a higher Opinion of the natural Capacities of the black Race, than I had ever before entertained. Their Apprehension seems as quick, their Memory as strong, and their Docility in every Respect equal to that of white Children."

If adult slaves were less capable than their masters, Franklin believed, the cause was to be found in the way they had been reared and treated all their lives, and not in any natural inferiority. Therefore, they should be accorded the same opportunities as anyone else to develop to their full potential.

In some respects, Benjamin Franklin was a man apart. He towered above virtually everyone he met in terms of intellect and creativity. Yet he did not regard his gifts as a license to take from others. Instead, he recognized dozens of practical ways to enrich the lives of ordinary people. He helped to build a democratic culture for the ages and tried to improve the lives of his neighbors in the moment. He seems to have arisen every morning animated by the question, "What can I do to be of service to my fellow humans?"

six

ALEXANDER
Service through Suffering

OUR BODIES MAKE POSSIBLE MANY FORMS OF PLEASURE. CONSIDER THE senses, each with its own delights. Smell—the aroma of fresh-baked bread, or the scent of our beloved. Taste—savory meats, tangy citrus fruits, and the sweetness of a freshly roasted ear of corn. Touch—the warmth of a parent's embrace, or the thrill of holding hands for the first time. Sound—the whispering of a cherished phrase between lovers, or the spirit's soaring through great music. And sight— which brings us both the cherished face of a child and the glorious hues of sunrise and sunset.

Yet the body that makes possible so many delights can also serve as the instrument of torment. Through smell we can be subjected to the putrid; through taste, the nauseating; through touch, all manner of pains; through sound, cacophony and the confirmation of a dreaded catastrophe; and through sight, horrible images we wish we had never seen.

Under certain circumstances, the body becomes a disturbing liability. Consider someone traveling in an aircraft experiencing severe turbulence, or a person who has fallen down a shaft head-first and become wedged in it. The same can be said when we fall seriously ill or suffer a grievous injury, or when we are forcibly detained or imprisoned. The body can drag us down and constrain us. Our flesh is our vulnerability.

Some among us seem cursed because they have known many of these forms of suffering. They have been removed from everything and everyone they love. They have been placed in prisons, beyond whose walls they have no hope of venturing. They have been tortured by deprivation and beatings and worse. They have been threatened with execution by hanging or firing squad.

In some cases, such deprivations of liberty are seen as just. The incarcerated have been judged guilty of a heinous crime, for which a thirst for retribution or justice leads others to confine them or do them bodily harm. In other cases, however, such suffering cannot be justified. It may even represent an extreme form of injustice—the punishment of the good simply because of the threat they are perceived to pose to the wicked. History and literature are full of tales of individuals who have been unjustly detained, imprisoned, tortured, and even executed for crimes they did not commit, precisely because unjust people wanted them out of the way.

Particularly inspiring are cases in which, despite suffering such injustices, released victims do not seek to inflict similar torments on their tormentors. One shining twentieth-century example is that of Nelson Mandela, who spent twenty-seven years in South African prisons, yet emerged a gentler man who sought not vengeance, but justice through the establishment of a truth and reconciliation commission. In other cases, victims of such wrongs have emerged from prison not burning with hatred but with a profound sense of calling to share the truth of what they and they fellow inmates experienced.

Alexander

One such case rests on an almost unimaginable set of circumstances. A man named Alexander had for some time noticed a swelling in his groin. Like many people, his first response was to ignore it. Yet it kept getting bigger, and eventually it grew to the size of a lemon. Finally, he sought medical attention. The doctors who examined him determined that the lesion should be surgically removed. He left the operation assuming that he had been cured.

Several years later, however, he began to develop pains in his abdomen, which gradually worsened until they became excruciating. He could barely sleep, and he soon lost his appetite for food. As the weeks passed, he became thinner and thinner. The doctors thought that he was probably suffering from gastritis or some other intestinal disorder.

When the passage of time did not bring any improvement, Alexander was sent to a hospital in another town. There, X-ray examination revealed a tumor the size of a large apple in the back of his abdomen. The doctors told him that the lesion might a malignant cancer of the lymph glands. Only later did they determine that it was in fact a form of testicular cancer that had spread from his groin to lymph nodes in his abdomen.

The doctors prescribed radiation therapy, hoping that the tumor would shrink rapidly and perhaps disappear altogether. On the day Alexander arrived at the hospital for treatment, the pain was so severe that he could not stand, sit, or lie down for more than a few minutes, making sleep nearly impossible. He received more than four dozen daily radiation treatments. Although the doctors had given him only a one-in-three chance of surviving the cancer and its treatment, the tumor responded well to the radiation and shrank substantially. Months later, after additional treatments, the disease seemed to have disappeared.

Yet cancer was not the beginning of Alexander's ordeal, nor would it be the end. In the years leading up to his diagnosis, he had suffered from a different yet equally toxic form of dis-ease, a nightmare dominated by persecution and imprisonment. And now that his treatment was complete, he was not returning to a loving family, a comfortable home, a well-paying job, or a secure place in the community. Instead, he was being sent back to exile in a distant land, cut off from those he loved.

Alexander was not an American living in the twenty-first century, but a citizen of the Union of Soviet Socialist Republics living in the mid-twentieth century, whose life had been filled with misfortune. For this was Alexander Solzhenitsyn.

Born in 1918 in the midst of World War I, his mother, who came from a privileged background, had married a young officer in the imperial army. Soon after learning that she was pregnant, her husband was killed in a hunting accident.

The war and subsequent revolution in Russia led to a reversal of the family's fortunes, and Solzhenitsyn was raised in humble circumstances by his widowed mother and his aunt. But despite their poverty, his mother encouraged him to read widely and pursue science, and she instilled in him a deep faith in the Russian Orthodox Church. He displayed a keen intelligence and went on to study at university. There he soon turned away from his mother's faith and embraced communism.

During World War II, Solzhenitsyn rose to the command of an anti-artillery battery and was decorated for bravery. Yet before long he began to entertain doubts about the Soviet regime. His doubts heightened when he witnessed his comrades committing atrocities against the Germans, including pillaging towns and raping women. He shared his doubts about Stalinism in a letter to a former schoolmate. The letter was intercepted, leading to his arrest and subsequent internment in a labor camp with a sentence of eight years.

Initially, Solzhenitsyn was moved from camp to camp, forced to perform manual labor like all the other prisoners. Eventually, however, his intellectual gifts became apparent, and he was sent to a special research facility, where conditions were somewhat less harsh. Still later he was sent to a special camp for political prisoners, where he worked as a bricklayer and oversaw foundry work. It was here, at the special camp, that the tumor was removed from his groin.

Three years later, Solzhenitsyn's eight-year sentence was over, and he was sent to a distant town in the east, in "perpetual exile," where he expected to live out the remainder of his life. But his cancer recurred, leading to the excruciating abdominal pains that landed him in the cancer hospital for radiation treatments. Though the radiation therapy relieved his physical suffering, he still faced the prospect of many years in exile.

Over the course of the decade or so that marked his imprisonment, exile, and treatment for cancer, Solzhenitsyn's views on the purpose of life were dramatically transformed. He came to regard Marxism as untenable and found himself returning to the Christian faith of his childhood. Then, thanks to the political reforms of Nikita Khrushchev during the 1950s, Solzhenitsyn was freed from exile and absolved of his crimes against the state.

Solzhenitsyn could find work only as a schoolteacher. He labored during the day in the classroom, but he devoted his nights to writing because he was burning with a need to capture in words what he had witnessed and experienced over the course of his tragic odyssey. By his own admission, "I was convinced that I would never see a single line of mine in print" and "scarcely dared to let even close acquaintances read anything for fear of discovery." Yet he continued to write furiously, impelled by an unseen force to share the stories of his fellow prisoners.

Eventually, after many nights of soul searching, Solzhenitsyn approached the editor of a prominent literary magazine with one of his manuscripts, an account of a single day in the life of a prisoner, inspired by his own early years of internment. To his surprise, *One Day in the Life of Ivan Denisovich* was soon under review by Khrushchev himself, who allowed it to be published. The work became a best seller and was quickly adopted as required reading in Soviet schools, where it served as a warning against the abuses of Stalinism.

Solzhenitsyn then attempted to publish a second work inspired by his experiences as a cancer patient, *Cancer Ward*. This time, however, the writer's union deemed the work too overtly political and denied publication. Soon thereafter Khrushchev fell from power, and the political climate in the Soviet Union underwent a dramatic change. Publication of Solzhenitsyn's work ceased, his papers were seized, and he was designated a nonperson. Thereafter, he wrote only in secrecy, but he continued to write, and his output was vast.

Solzhenitsyn's book *The Gulag Archipelago* ranks as one of the greatest works of twentieth-century literature. He composed in constant fear of detection, its seven parts so closely guarded that they were never united at any one time. The book weaves together history, personal narrative, and philosophical investigation, as well as the testimonies of 256 prisoners. It has sold tens of millions of copies in dozens of languages and represents one of the most politically transformative works of literature in any age.

When Solzhenitsyn died of heart failure at the age of eighty-nine in 2008, he was not a popular man in many circles. The Soviet Union had imprisoned him, censored his works, expelled him, and even attempted to assassinate him. His popularity in the West waned after he offered religiously inspired critiques of Western materialism and purposelessness, warning that "men have forgotten God." He was variously branded a reactionary, a theocrat, and even an anti-Semite.

Cancer Ward

Perhaps no book written in the twentieth century has done more than Solzhenitsyn's *Cancer Ward* to illuminate the relationship between the health of the individual, the health of the community, and the role that each can play in destroying or enhancing the other. It explores health in its many different senses—the biological, psychological, and moral health of individual human beings, as well as the economic, political, and spiritual health of an entire society.

In every chapter, Solzhenitsyn puts service to the test. Do we serve ourselves, at the expense of others and the community? Do we lay down our lives in service to others, to the community, or to an idea? The question is not whether or not to serve, for every human life plays itself out in service to something; instead, at issue is the nature of the god or gods we serve and the human consequences of these choices.

Though not an autobiography, there is no denying that *Cancer Ward* is a powerfully autobiographical work. Completed in 1966, it was banned in the Soviet Union the following year. It tells the story of a group of patients in a provincial hospital in Soviet Asia in 1955. Like the author, the book's main character, Oleg Kostoglotov, has recently been released from a Soviet labor camp, having been convicted of counterrevolutionary activities.

The cancer ward is a drab and underresourced place, where patients undergo barbaric tests and treatments. One patient, Rusanov, is a bureaucrat responsible for hunting down enemies of the state. He thinks he is better than the others, expects special treatment, and never feels a sense of kinship with anyone. Unable to believe that he is afflicted with a potentially fatal illness, he eventually leaves the hospital unchanged, wrongly supposing that he is cured.

Other patients include a student seeking to address social problems who has a leg amputated, a young geologist who had hoped to advance knowledge before learning that his cancer is incurable, a young gymnast who must undergo a mastectomy, a peasant who has been paralyzed by spinal cancer, and a librarian tortured by the fact that he failed to speak out against the political regime before it was too late.

The staff of the clinic includes a radiologist who has treated hundreds of cancer patients but cannot bear to see her own illness; several incompetent nurses and doctors who cannot be removed from their posts; and Vera, the middle-aged doctor who treats Oleg with great tenderness. He imagines spending the rest of his life with her, but at the novel's end their union is prevented by his desire not to burden her.

The kinship between *Cancer Ward* and Leo Tolstoy's *The Death of Ivan Ilych* is obvious. In both, a protagonist is diagnosed with a lethal illness that gradually sucks the life from him, and in both cases, the attitudes of the afflicted and those around him provide profound insights into enduring questions of life and death. In Tolstoy's work, however, the protagonist dies, while in Solzhenitsyn's, the man lives—though for what?

There is a strong kinship as well between the life of Solzhenitsyn and that of another great Russian novelist, Fyodor Dostoyevsky. Dostoyevsky also felt that his life had been transformed by suffering, including imprisonment. He too came to regard his incarceration as a form of education that taught him the real nature and value of freedom and the difference between what is truly admirable and lamentable in human life.

Writing in a partly autobiographical vein in the novel *The Idiot*, Dostoyevsky describes a scene, reminiscent of his own life, of being led to execution for political offenses: "This man was led out along with others on to a scaffold and had his sentence of death read out to him. He was dying at 27, healthy and strong. He said that nothing was more terrible at that moment than the nagging thought: 'What if I didn't have to die! I would turn every minute into an age, nothing would be wasted, every minute would be accounted for!' About twenty minutes later a reprieve was read out and a milder form of punishment substituted."

Spending years in labor camps, nearly wasting away from cancer, or staring down a firing squad can produce a dramatic reordering of one's priorities in life. By placing everything at risk, such experiences clarify the difference between the means of living and the end of life. Money and power may be useful in many circumstances, but in the face of death, their limits become painfully obvious, as does the futility of a life devoted to them.

It is no surprise that Solzhenitsyn's *Cancer Ward* has little good to say about wealth and power, which so often function as human corruptors. What is surprising, however, is that even happiness seems unable to serve as a substitute. Being happy is no good if our satisfaction requires the suffering of others. The worst of the cancer ward's patients are the ones who look for happiness by ignoring those around them.

Hence the *Cancer Ward* is not about prosperity in any conventional sense. Those who prosper in the material sense often become progressively more insulated from the experiences of those around them, to the point that, like the character of the political officer, they despise them. Oleg's strength of character is grounded not in his adherence to any ideology, but in his rejection of all ideology, his steadfast refusal to see those around him as anything other than who they really are. He is loyal, first and foremost, to truth.

One of Oleg's friends reminds him that it is possible to find happiness even in exile, as long as we properly understand the real nature of happiness: "It is not our level of prosperity that makes for happiness but the kinship of heart to heart and the way we look at the world. Both attitudes lie within our power, so that a man is happy so long as he chooses to be happy, and no one can stop him." The key is to regard our fellow human beings with a sense of kinship and to seek out all that is good, true, and beautiful in the world.

Some people think they can calculate their prosperity by the number of things they can buy or the number of people they can fire or send to prison, but to prosper in this sense is to become mired in a pit of self-loathing. Exercising such control over others entangles a person in a web of corruption, draining away humanity.

It would be foolish to contest the realization that virtually everything we have can be taken way from us: our homes, our possessions, our titles, and even our freedom to move about and associate with those we choose. But no one can stop the happiness of the person whose eyes and heart are always searching for the true and good. Only when the layers of falsehood and corruption have been stripped away can we perceive the beauty underneath.

Cancer Ward provides a beautiful example of such a human being in the person of a "short, narrow-shouldered woman in a white coat," a bespectacled orderly who works the nightshift. Her name is Elizaveta Anatolyevna. She is in most respects a nobody, unnoticed by both the patients and the staff of the cancer ward. One night, when Oleg is overwhelmed by a sense of hopelessness, he spies her reading under a lamp:

> During the two months Oleg had spent in the hospital, this painstaking orderly with the quick, intelligent expression had often crawled under their beds to wash the floor while they lay above her. She would always move Oleg's books, which he kept secretly in the dark depths under his bed, carefully to one side, and never cursed him for it. She wiped the wall panels, cleaned the spittoons and polished them until they shone. She distributed jars with labels to the patients. Anything heavy, inconvenient, or dirty that the nurses were not supposed to touch she had to carry to and fro.
>
> The more uncomplainingly she worked, the less notice everyone took of her. As the two-thousand-year-old saying goes, you can have eyes and still not see.

What she is reading, we do not yet know, and she never espouses what we might call her "philosophy of life." It is not one she articulates but one she lives, and it shines through in everything she does. She carries out her duties without complaint. She does not draw attention to herself. She treats others with dignity. The key is not what others see, or fail to see, in her, but rather what she sees in them— an opportunity to serve.

Her life is hard, yet she bears the burden lightly. She seems to have little to rejoice over or look forward to in life, yet her quick, intelligent eyes are not avaricious or covetous of praise. She spends her nights surrounded by human beings gripped by suffering, surrounded by foul sights and sounds and odors, yet she betrays no distaste. What does she see in this miserable place and the sufferings of these miserable human beings?

> A hard life improves the vision. There were some in the hospital who immediately recognized one another for what they were. Although in no way distinguished by uniform, shoulder insignia, or armband, they could still recognize each other easily. It was as if they bore some luminous insignia on their foreheads, or stigmata on their feet and palms. (In fact there were plenty of clues: a word dropped here and there; the way it was spoken; a tightening of the lips between words; a smile while others were serious or while others laughed.) The Uzbeks and the Kara-Kalpaks had no difficulty recognizing one another in the clinic, nor did those who had once lived in the shadows of barbed wire.
>
> Oleg and she had long ago recognized each other, and since then they had always greeted one another understandingly. There had never been a chance for them to have a talk, however.
>
> Oleg walked up to her table, slapping with his slippers so as not to alarm her. "Good evening, Elizaveta Anatolyevna."

She was reading without glasses. She turned her head in some indefinably different way from usual, ready to answer to the call of duty.

"Good evening." She smiled with all the dignity of a lady of a certain age receiving a welcome guest under her own roof.

Agreeably and without hurry they regarded each other. The look meant that they were always ready to give one another help.

But there was no help either of them could give.

This woman works the night shift scrubbing floors and emptying bedpans in a provincial cancer hospital. She has no money to her name, lacks the authority to bark out orders to anyone, and is not even recognized by the people she works with and for. She is, in most conventional respects, a nobody, a nonperson, occupying the same rung on society's ladder that Oleg himself has been reduced to.

She is not, physically at least, capable of bearing much of a burden. She is small and near-sighted, requiring glasses except when she is reading. She reads because it gets her close to things, close enough to see them clearly without need of correction. While others shirk their work or while away their shift in amusements, she completes her duties promptly so she can read.

And what is she reading? It turns out to be a work by the French novelist Claude Farrère, whose most famous book was *La Bataille* (The Battle). A romantic novel set in Nagasaki, it tells the story of a young Japanese couple whose lives are torn apart by their country's war with Russia, presenting the war from the perspective of the underdog Japanese. It is, in other words, a depiction of love between two overmatched people who are at war with Russia.

It turns out that Elizaveta and her family were exiled for counterrevolutionary activities. Her daughter died in exile, and after the war the family moved to the hospital town, where her husband was arrested a second time. "As for who was punished for whom," she says, "I haven't any idea." None of the family members was guilty—or perhaps they were all guilty. She and Oleg share the same guilt as well—the guilt of seeing things as they really are, and not as those in power would like them to appear.

Elizaveta's modest dignity contrasts sharply with that of the family of the party bureaucrat Rusanov, who on admission to the cancer ward refuses to believe his diagnosis and on discharge stubbornly refuses to believe that he has not been cured. He is sick in body, but also in spirit, in ways that no microscope or CT scan can reveal: "The Rusanovs loved the People, their great People. They served the People and were ready to give their lives for the People. But as the years went by they found themselves less and less able to tolerate actual human beings, those obstinate creatures who were always resistant, refusing to do what they were told to, and besides, demanding something for themselves."

Unlike Elizaveta, the Rusanovs think themselves better than everyone else. They are unwilling to serve anyone. Far from serving, they are in fact filled with fear. Rusanov himself is tortured by dreams that a man he betrayed many years before will reappear and confront him. He has sacrificed countless others, including many he recognizes as innocent, in hopes of advancing his own career. Yet he cannot understand his own son's resolute refusal to follow his father and strike a similar bargain.

Looking at life from the vantage point of the cancer ward, it becomes clear to Oleg that some things in life are more important than life itself—among them, the preservation of humanity: "Should a man, to preserve his life, pay everything that gives life color, scent, and excitement? Can one accept a life of digestion, respiration, muscular and brain activity—and nothing more? Become a walking blueprint? Is this not an exorbitant price? Is it not mockery? Should one pay? Seven years in the army and seven years in the camp—twice that mythical or biblical term, then to be deprived of the ability to tell what is a man and what is a woman—is that price not extortionate?"

It is not when human beings are at their seeming best—wallets fat with cash, flaunting lofty titles, names on everyone's lips, and full of satisfaction to be counted among the worthiest—that their humanity is most clearly discernible. In fact, the opposite is more often the case. It is when we have been stripped of such accretions that we can see most clearly what we really are.

To lose sight of this reality is, from Solzhenitsyn's point of view, simply too high a price to pay for any reward. When we lose our humanity, we lose our very selves, and no amount of wealth, power, fame, or pleasure can restore us to life. It is in the cancer ward, when we are confronted with the prospect of our own mortality, beyond which nothing we are proud of can be carried with us, that we see what is really worth living for.

Of his own trials—imprisonment, exile, ostracism, cancer, and attempted murder—Solzhenitsyn wrote: "When at the end of jail, on top of everything else, I was placed with cancer, then I was finally cleansed and came back to a deep awareness of God and a deep understanding of life. From that time, I formed essentially into who I am now."

seven

JOHN
Service through Education

THERE IS A TENDENCY AMONG SOME ADULTS TO SPEAK OF THE PLAY OF children condescendingly, as though if only the young could see themselves, they would be ashamed. Girls caring for baby dolls and playing house, boys playing cops and robbers or roughhousing in the grass—no self-respecting adult would be caught dead engaging in such fanciful and idle pursuits.

I remember as a college biology student, having been taught that life is about survival and reproduction, attempting to reconcile the exigencies of existence with the frivolity of play. How can young organisms afford to expend so much energy on pursuits that contribute nothing to their prospects for securing themselves and propelling their genes into the next generation? In some more adventurous or perhaps foolhardy cases, such as kids jumping from a bridge into a creek, the young even put their lives on the line. A kid who dove headfirst without first checking for underwater hazards could end up paralyzed, or worse.

But then I thought, perhaps such play does contribute to biological fitness by fostering skills that will someday play a crucial role in perpetuating the species. For example, playing with baby dolls might help make a child a better parent, and playing ball might foster better hand-eye coordination needed to hunt game. Over the years, however, I have become more suspicious of survival and reproduction as life's sole purposes.

Looking back on my own play and observing that of my children and grandchildren, it seems to me that play might constitute its own reward. It can conjure a powerful form of camaraderie, the sharing of experience for its own sake. It presents us with challenges to surmount, drawing on virtues such as courage, fairness, and self-control. And it brings a special kind of joy—the magic of moving purposefully through space.

What is the purpose of jumping rope, building a fort, or playing a game of basketball? For that matter, what is the purpose of a painting, a symphony, or a novel? Must we contort the round abundance of play to make it fit into the square hole of biological utility? Or dare we suppose that the joy we find in it is purpose enough? Might it even be appropriate to say that creation itself delights in play? What if it is less true to say that we seek out play in order to prepare ourselves for survival than to say that we seek to survive in order to have more opportunities to play?

In an era when sports have become particularly commercialized and commodified, the temptation to emphasize the utility of play becomes especially acute. Perhaps youth sports exist in order to select out and develop those rare individuals who have what it takes to excel at the highest level of sport—competing in the Olympics and earning huge sums of money as professional athletes. Yet many who care about sports are less tempted to agonize over the fate of would-be superstars who never "make it" than to bemoan the corruption of the amateur tradition that money has wrought.

There are, after all, people who play sports, coach sports, and love sports not because they expect it to build their wealth or contribute to their lives in any utilitarian sense, but simply because they love the game. They love to play, they love to see the game played well, and they love helping to bring out the best in others on the field of play. From a makeshift goal in a child's backyard to a school or municipal playing field to a luxury professional sports arena, such people see the chance to play as a chance to experience a grace in motion for which the human soul longs.

The greatest coach in the history of American sport preferred to be regarded as a teacher. Although he originally hoped to be a civil engineer, he decided in college to switch his career to teaching English, and all his life he quoted poems he learned as an adolescent. One of his favorites was this:

No written word, nor spoken plea
Can teach our youth what they should be.
Nor all the books on all the shelves,
It's what the teachers are themselves

Though not a perfect human being, the coach earned the respect, admiration, and devotion of generations of basketball players. He did so not by teaching strategies or tactics or preaching a total dedication to winning, but by embodying essential lessons for life.

The coach was born in Hall, Indiana, in 1910. When he was eight years old, his family moved to Centerton, Indiana, where their property abutted that of another Indiana basketball legend, Emmett B. "Branch" McCracken, who coached two Indiana University national championship teams and was inducted into the basketball Hall of Fame. When this coach was fourteen, the family moved to Martinsville, where he led his high school basketball team to three state championship games, winning All-State honors all three years.

In college, the coach played basketball at Purdue University, where he was named the nation's first three-time consensus All-American. One of these squads, which played in an era before a tournament determined the national championship, was later named national champion. Though only five feet, ten inches tall, he was known for extraordinary quickness, fierce determination, and a willingness to dive after any ball, which earned him the sobriquet "The India Rubber Man."

After graduating from college, he played professional basketball for several Midwestern teams, at one point using his underhand technique to sink a record 134 consecutive free throws. He then joined the US Navy, where an attack of appendicitis prevented him from serving in a post that suffered a devastating attack and might have cost him his life.

After the navy the coach became an English teacher and high school basketball and baseball coach, first in Dayton, Kentucky, and then in South Bend, Indiana. When his former high school coach left Indiana State Teachers College (now Indiana State University) in Terre Haute, he was appointed the new basketball coach. He also completed a master's degree in education there.

His Indiana State team received invitations to the 1947 and 1948 national tournaments in Kansas City, but he turned the first one down because the tournament refused to allow black players to suit up. The next year, the policy changed, and the coach fielded the first black player ever to appear in a national postseason basketball tournament.

Looking to leave Indiana State, he was recruited by the University of Minnesota and UCLA. He preferred the Minnesota position, but when a snowstorm prevented officials at Minnesota from reaching him by phone, he accepted the UCLA offer—a commitment he refused to back out of when he later learned what had happened.

Though life in Los Angeles initially did not suit him, his wife, or their two children, he enjoyed immediate triumph on the court, converting an unsuccessful team into the conference champion in his first year. Despite a growing record of success, his teams played for many years in a third-floor gymnasium that could accommodate only twenty-five hundred fans and had to be shared at practice time with teams from other sports.

Eventually, the coach's teams made it to the NCAA postseason tournament, where they achieved unparalleled success. Over twelve years during the 1960s and 1970s, they won a total of ten national championships, including a record eighty-eight consecutive games and seven consecutive titles. These championship teams featured very different rosters—one that included no player taller than six feet, five inches when other teams featured seven-foot centers.

The coach himself became the first person ever inducted into the basketball Hall of Fame as both a player and a coach. His name, of course, is John Wooden, and in 2009 *Sporting News* named him the greatest coach in the history of American sport.

John

Wooden's teams were known for their fast tempo of play and superb conditioning, which frequently enabled them to come from behind and win games in the final minutes. His players often described his practices as the most demanding experiences of their lives, each one programmed out in detail on three-by-five-inch cards.

Wooden believed in the fundamentals, to the point that he began practice every year by teaching players how to put on their shoes and socks, in part to help them avoid blisters. He had little to say to his players during games, believing that the lessons they needed to perform at their best had been instilled during practices. Team practices were the coach's business, but once the game began, Wooden believed, it was up to the players. This approach contrasted sharply with those of other coaches, many of whom insisted that their team execute the coach's plan down to the smallest detail.

Wooden viewed his emphasis on fundamentals not as a pattern to which every player needed to conform, but as a set of tools players needed to be able to exercise their own creativity and initiative as evolving situations on the court demanded. Wooden once claimed that he hoped to be as surprised as his team's opponents by what his players came up with when confronted by an unexpected challenge.

Seven Points

Wooden's philosophy of basketball education was firmly grounded in a philosophy of life that he learned at a young age from his father. When he graduated from grade school, his father gave him a wallet-sized card bearing a seven-point creed that Wooden kept with him throughout his life. Each time the card began to wear out, he made a new one. Although none of the seven points specifically pertains to basketball, they helped instill in Wooden a keen appetite for excellence, grounded in service to something beyond self:

1. Be true to yourself.
2. Make each day your masterpiece.
3. Help others.
4. Drink deeply from good books, especially the Bible.
5. Make friendship a fine art.
6. Build a shelter against a rainy day.
7. Pray for guidance and give thanks for your blessings every day.

These seven points comprise a fine introduction to Wooden's deep convictions concerning the connection between coming to life and serving others.

The first point, "Be true to yourself," is found in one of the most famous speeches in the history of drama, from Shakespeare's *Hamlet*:

> This above all—to thine own self be true;
> And it must follow, as the night the day,
> Thou canst not then be false to any man.

These words are spoken by Polonius, who is often portrayed as a bumbler and windbag. This has tended to undercut the credibility of these words, leading many people to regard them as hackneyed and not to be taken seriously. But coming from John Wooden, the injunction to be true to oneself takes on a different character.

As both a player and a coach, Wooden appeared to harbor a deep hunger for victory. Yet on a number of occasions at the height of his coaching career, he actually expressed relief that his team had lost a game. Perhaps the best-known such instance occurred in January 1974 in South Bend, Indiana, after Notre Dame snapped UCLA's unprecedented eighty-eight-game winning streak, which had carried on for nearly eleven hundred days.

As the streak grew longer, Wooden kept insisting that it was only a matter of time before it ended, and when it finally did, he was gracious in defeat, agreeing that the number-one ranking should go to Notre Dame. (It did not stay there long, however, as UCLA trounced the Fighting Irish by nineteen points a week later in Los Angeles.) The defeat provided the team with an opportunity to refocus attention on what really mattered—playing its best basketball.

From Wooden's point of view, being true to oneself had nothing to do with winning. As he often said, "Success comes not from victories, but from knowing that you did everything you could to be the best you could be." Wooden was referring not to a win-loss record, but to excellence, which he seems to have regarded as closely akin to authenticity.

Wooden thought most highly of the players who played closest to their full potential and did the most to bring out the best in the team—not those players who scored the most points or grabbed the most rebounds. Wooden was more concerned with what a player was capable of accomplishing based on his ability, and the degree to which he was able to make the most of the opportunity. This required self-knowledge—a deep understanding on the part of each player of his own capabilities and how they meshed with those of the other players on the court. When asked to name his favorite National Basketball Association player, Wooden named not the league's top scorer, but John Stockton, professional basketball's all-time assist leader.

Wooden's second point, "Make each day your masterpiece," has roots in the Roman poet Horace's famous aphorism, "Seize the day, putting very little trust in tomorrow." Wooden seems to have agreed with Horace's view that a great deal of energy and peace of mind can be wasted worrying about the future. It's more important to make each day count. Too often, Wooden believed, we are so engrossed in rethinking something that happened in the past or preoccupied by anxieties about the future that we fritter away the present, spending large stretches of our lives barely living at all.

Wooden carried this principle into the game of basketball. The injunction to make each day a masterpiece meant making each game, each play, and each action on the court—shooting, rebounding, passing, dribbling, setting a pick, and so forth—its own masterpiece. Wooden was not suggesting that his players disregard every minute but the present one. Instead, he was urging them to cultivate the art of *presence*, completely immersing themselves in the activity at hand. He was arguing against divided attention and in favor of complete dedication to the moment.

This aspect of Wooden is captured well in the reflections of one of his greatest players, Bill Walton: "He never talks about winning and losing but rather about the effort to win. He rarely talks about basketball but generally about life. He never talks about strategy, statistics, or plays but rather about people and character. And he never tires of telling us that once you become a good person, then you have a chance of becoming a good basketball player." Why wouldn't Wooden talk about shooting percentages or average rebounds per game? The answer, it seems, is that focusing on statistics does nothing to help a person perform better. A player cannot excel by focusing on a statistic, because there is no statistically executable action in a basketball game.

In other words, Wooden wanted his players, and his students in the classroom, to focus on what they could actually *do*, not on what they *wished* would happen. There is a difference between excellence and good luck, and while Wooden did not disregard the role of fortune or divine providence in the outcome of events, he believed that we human beings are called to maintain a focus on the things at which we can excel.

Whether a particular pass reaches its target, a team wins a game, or a person prospers in life depends on a host of factors outside the control of any individual, but people can do their best to ensure that if they are successful, they will have done everything possible to have earned that success.

Wooden's third and most cogent point is simply, "Help others." There are multiple reasons someone might offer such advice. Thomas Hobbes, the seventeenth-century English philosopher who regarded humanity's natural state as one of solitude and isolation, advocated helping others as a sort of insurance policy. Others might be more likely to render aid to a person who had once helped them. Helping others might also advance our own interests—building relationships and loyalties that can be useful in promoting success down the line.

Wooden, however, regarded helping others in a quite different light. For him, the reason for rendering aid to others was not to build up a bag of chips and IOUs that could be called in once the need arose. He often said that it is impossible to live a perfect day "unless you do something for someone who will never be able to repay you."

He explicitly said, "someone who will *never* be able to repay you." The idea is not just that a person is incapable of paying you back at the moment, but that such repayment is in principle impossible. In other words, the help needs to be intended not as an enlightened form of self-interest, but strictly for the benefit of the recipient of the aid. This is service in its purest and most noble form—the kind grounded solely in the welfare of another person.

One of the traits of a basketball player that Wooden esteemed most highly was selflessness. A selfless player took a shot or made a great play only when it served the interests of *the team*. The selfless player thought not about how many points he was scoring or whether he would be named most valuable player, but how he could help *the team* perform at its best. Wooden and many of his players understood that the greatest sense of fulfillment the basketball court has to offer comes from promoting the excellence of the team, not from shining as an individual.

As Wooden himself liked to say, a player imbued with this spirit would exhibit not merely a *willingness* to sacrifice his personal interest for the welfare of the team, but a positive *eagerness* to do so. As long as we assume that we are Hobbesian hermits, leading "solitary, poor, nasty, brutish and short" lives locked in a zero-sum game where any individual's gain requires another's loss, the impulse to help others seems ill-advised, perhaps even lamentable. Once we understand, however, as did Wooden, that we are in fact members of a team—or more broadly speaking, part of larger whole—then the possibility emerges that serving others can make everyone better off.

Wooden's fourth and central point, "Drink deeply from good books," was reflected in his lifelong love of reading. Visitors to his tiny condominium in Encino, California, often expressed surprise when they found no shrine to basketball or coaching. Instead, Wooden's home was full of books. In fact, he was rarely seen without a book ready to hand. And these were not basketball books but the sorts of books you might expect to find in the home of an English teacher, which was largely how Wooden thought of himself.

Wooden believed that a basketball player's performance is limited by his grasp of the fundamentals of the game, just as he believed that excellence in life is limited by the ideas with which we live. To lead a good life, a person needs to understand what life is about, to be able to distinguish between what is of greater and lesser importance. The trappings of success—money, power, and fame—are useless, or even harmful, to people whose lack of a sound moral compass prevents them from appreciating their limitations. From Wooden's point of view, it would be better to be judged a failure yet be a good person than to appear wildly successful but be corrupt inside.

Wooden believed that we are as good as the books we read, and he surrounded himself with good books. And by far the best book, in his view, was the Bible. He read it daily, and his favorite passage was 1 Corinthians 13, the so-called love chapter. He often reminded both himself and his players that basketball is not life's ultimate good: "It is of little importance in comparison to the total life we live. There is only one kind of life that truly wins, and that is the one that places faith in the hands of the Savior. Until that is done, we are on an aimless course that runs in circles and goes nowhere." To help others become the best people they are capable of being—this was Wooden's ultimate good. "Material possessions, winning scores, and great reputations are meaningless in the eyes of the Lord," he said, "because he knows what we really are and that is all that matters."

Some may reject or even resent Wooden's emphasis on faith, but it is impossible to understand what he did or who he was without grasping this aspect of the man. For Wooden, faith was not a costume people don to appear better than they are. Nor did he see it as a collection of rules for living that determined a person's eternal fate. Rather, he regarded his Christian faith as the most accurate description of the world we inhabit, a world ultimately governed less by rules of cause and effect than by the love of God. As Wooden saw it, the very existence of the world is a clear indication of that love, and our mission in life is to focus that love by caring for others. This, and not winning, Wooden believed, is the real source of joy in human life.

Wooden's fifth point was "Make friendship a fine art." His former players frequently reported that they did not feel like his friends while they were playing for him. He did not spend a lot of free time with them, nor did he get involved in their personal lives. He thought that he could be most effective and bring out the best in them by being their teacher, not their pal.

Yet once players graduated, their relationship with Wooden changed. He took a much greater interest in their professional and family lives and did what he could to help them find opportunities for success in life. One sports writer who interviewed Wooden was surprised to discover that the coach could name the current location, career, and family circumstances of 172 of 180 of the players who had been part of his championship teams. He stayed in touch with them because he cared about them, and this dedication was not confined to his most recent and most successful teams.

I spoke to a man who had been a member of one of Wooden's baseball teams when he was teaching English and coaching basketball in South Bend, Indiana. The man reported that when Wooden saw him, the coach recognized him immediately, although the man hadn't seen or heard from Wooden in decades. Wooden even recalled that the man had been the team's third baseman.

The point is not that Wooden had an extraordinary memory for names and faces. It is rather that he cared about his players, his "students," to whom he remained dedicated for the rest of his life. Wooden once explained his love for his players by invoking the memory of the great University of Chicago football coach Amos Alonzo Stagg:

> He had many players he didn't like and didn't respect, but he loved them just the same. I hope my players know that I love them all. There were times I didn't like them. There were times I didn't like my own children, but it never had anything to do with my love for them. If people want to be basketball players, if they know you care for them, if you're not a dictator and if you make them feel that they're working with you, not for you, I don't know what I couldn't do today. Stagg also said that you couldn't tell whether you had a successful season until 20 years or so after they've graduated.

Wooden saw each season and each playing career as part of a longer life trajectory, and it was in large part for life after basketball that he saw himself as preparing his players.

Wooden spoke with pride about his players, but not for the reasons we might expect. When he was giving talks about his philosophy of coaching, he frequently highlighted players whom many of the members of his audience had never heard of—rather than the ones who had scored the most points or secured the most lucrative professional careers. He would point to a player who never started but was now enjoying a happy and successful life as a partner in a prominent local law firm. His pride was rooted less in how many championships players had helped the team to win—in many cases, he was referring to players who had never been part of the starting lineup—and more in who they had become as human beings.

Wooden's sixth point—"Build a shelter against a rainy day"—was powerfully shaped by his family's humble circumstances. He grew up in difficult economic times, and his parents lost their farm and had to seek employment in the town of Martinsville. Wooden also suffered defeats and injuries as a player that served as powerful reminders that winning and losing are not always in the control of any team, coach, or player. You can perform at your absolute best and still lose. For all his greatness, Wooden and his college squad from Purdue would never stand a chance against one of his UCLA championship teams.

This sense that the tables could turn and everything be lost often puzzled Wooden's players. Many came from more fortunate circumstances, had always thought of themselves as the very best in the game, and looked forward to long and lucrative careers in professional basketball. When Wooden's best teams were winning, squad members expressed exasperation that the coach wouldn't relax and allow the team to enjoy its success. But from Wooden's point of view, winning was never assured, and only by remaining totally focused and dedicated could the team perform to its full potential—regardless of whether or not it happened to be scoring more points than the opponents.

Some opposing coaches explained Wooden's success in terms of divine providence—that the clean-living, church-going, Bible-quoting coach was God's favorite. But Wooden believed that God's ways are inscrutable and humans are fallen creatures. Furthermore, human beings can never completely insulate themselves from misfortune. The only reasonable response to such circumstances, Wooden would say, is to work hard. You might not be able to win, but you can do everything possible to give it your best shot. Even in defeat, you will know that you gave it all you had.

Wooden's final point—"Pray for guidance and give thanks for your blessings every day"—was the most explicitly religious of them all. Some of his players, such as Bill Walton, were deeply immersed in other spiritual practices, such as transcendental meditation, but Wooden had little doubt about the best form of quiet reflection—prayer.

Wooden's Christian faith defined him as a person. After winning a national championship, he would not race off to some amusement park or tropical resort, but take his grandchildren out for ice cream and then attend weekly worship services. He did this not in an attempt to remain in divine good graces, but as a sincere expression of gratitude.

For Wooden, the basketball court was a microcosm of human life and as good a learning environment as any for what it takes to be human. Some days the passes would find their mark, and the shots would drop into the basket; but other days things would not go so well. While UCLA trounced many opponents, the team also had a reputation for coming from behind and prevailing in close games. Wooden credited such performances to strong schooling in the fundamentals and superior physical conditioning, but he also recognized that forces were at work on a basketball court that he could not control, and in some cases could not even understand.

Giving thanks to God for a well-played game was the most appropriate form of celebration. Wooden did not suppose that God was watching every shot and deciding which ones should drop in. God was instead the ground of life and creation and had shaped the conditions under which the likes of Isaac Newton, for instance, could devise a theory of gravity or James Naismith could invent the game of basketball. Divine grace made it possible for young men to express such poise, fluidity, skill, and harmony on the court. Wooden could serve in cultivating such excellence, but most of the credit for it, he believed, belonged elsewhere.

eight

BILL

Service through Commerce

PROGRESS ALONG SOME PATHWAYS IN LIFE CAN BE DIFFICULT TO ASSESS, but commerce is generally not considered one of them. In the buying and selling of goods and services, the marketplace provides a relatively clear indicator of the value of what is being exchanged—purchase price—and the level at which each seller is performing—profit. When the system is working properly, merchants who provide high-value products tend to make money. Over time, those who make money consistently accumulate wealth and those who fail to generate a profit are driven out of business.

In many minds, the world of commerce is strongly distinguished from the world of charitable giving, or philanthropy. Commerce, so the conventional account goes, happens in the "for-profit" sector of the economy, while philanthropy is confined to the "nonprofit sector." Actors in the for-profit sector are thought to have one motive—to make money or increase shareholder value. And keeping score is relatively simple—those who perform the best generate the most wealth. The so-called nonprofit sector is trickier. In it, profit and the accumulation of wealth cannot, by definition, be the goal. In fact, the tax code defines nonprofit corporations in part by the fact that they do not distribute profits to shareholders.

This makes keeping score a good bit more difficult, and many nonprofits evaluate their performance by less clearly defined measures such as "impact." How do we know whether nonprofit organizations are having an impact, what the magnitude of that impact is, and whether the people they serve are generally better off because of their efforts?

Surveying the differences between for-profit and nonprofit organizations, a business-minded friend of mine once commented, "If the Ford Motor Company operated like the Ford Foundation, they would still be making Edsels." His point was that, without the discipline of the marketplace to weed out activities that are of little or no value—or in some cases, even harmful—nonprofit organizations might end up supporting doubtful programs and projects and persist in doing so long past the time when a for-profit corporation would have changed course.

This criticism is a bit unfair. After all, there is a kind of discipline in the non-profit world, at least among organizations that must raise funds to support their activities. If a philanthropic organization that depends on fund-raising is not meeting the needs of its constituency, it will soon find itself without the resources necessary to continue its work. Of course, this is not necessarily true for organizations that are under no pressure to raise funds, such as endowment-supported foundations, which theoretically can carry on performing poorly in perpetuity.

The key problem, however, is not how to ensure the accountability of philanthropic organizations, but whether the distinction between for-profit and nonprofit organizations is really so definitive. Who is to say that for-profit organizations are, at least in comparison to nonprofit ones, necessarily greedy and rapacious? Might there be cases in which for-profit organizations operate by equally philanthropic principles and generate as great a net benefit as nonprofit organizations?

My business-minded friend offered a similar opinion. "Many famous philanthropists," he said, "did more to promote human welfare through the activities of their for-profit companies than they ever did or ever will do through the good works of their foundations." He meant that the products and services such companies produced, the jobs they created, and the wealth their activities generated made a bigger difference for more people than the gifts bestowed by their foundations.

My friend's perspective seems to echo that of a medieval text on philanthropy, often referred to as Rambam's Ladder. Written in the twelfth century by the Jewish physician, philosopher, and rabbi Maimonides (who was also called Rambam), the eight-rung ladder provides a hierarchical account of different forms of giving arranged according to such factors as whether the donor gives grudgingly or willingly and whether the identity of the donor or recipient is known. Of all forms of charity, Maimonides ranks highest the type in which the donor finds the recipient employment, makes the recipient a loan, or enters into a partnership with the recipient.

Why would Maimonides put what appear to be business relationships of the sort we usually associate with for-profit organizations above those linked with nonprofits—namely, gift giving? Because when a giver finds a recipient employment, makes a loan, or enters into a partnership, writes Maimonides, he or she does so in order to "strengthen" the recipient until that person no longer needs to be "dependent on others." The implication is that independence is so preferable to dependence that it trumps all other factors in giving.

In ranking what amount to business relationships over charitable ones, Maimonides highlights the connection between self-sufficiency and self-respect. If people are in desperate need of food or shelter, it is better that they receive such necessities as gifts than die. But better still is helping them to become self-sufficient so that they can provide for themselves and their families. If they learn to fend for themselves, they might even become givers in their own right.

What Maimonides is referring to is feasible. I have seen it with my own eyes. And what I have seen calls into question, at least to some degree, the widely accepted distinction between for-profit and nonprofit organizations, at least in terms of their capacities to do good and make a difference. An old proverb often attributed to Lao-Tze says, "Give a man a fish and you feed him for a day; teach a man to fish and you feed him for a lifetime." In some cases—perhaps many—providing the means for self-sufficiency can provide greater benefit than ongoing gift giving.

Case in point: Bill Cook and his company the Cook Group. I choose this example because I am particularly familiar with it. Cook built his business in Bloomington, Indiana, which is close to my workplace in Indianapolis. Moreover, his business is based in the manufacture of medical devices that I use frequently in caring for patients. To learn about the Cook story, I met Cook before his death in 2011, and interviewed members of his family, colleagues, and friends. Cook's outlook on these matters illuminates key features of the potentially synergistic relationship between commerce and service.

Starting out in a two-bedroom apartment with a modest financial investment, Cook built a business that now employs more than thirteen thousand people around the world, creating the world's largest privately held medical device manufacturer and generating a personal fortune valued in the billions of dollars. His objective, however, was not primarily to make money, but to make a difference, in part by enabling the people he worked with to serve patients and their communities.

William Alfred "Bill" Cook (1931–2011) was born in Mattoon, Illinois, and grew up in the Illinois town of Canton. In high school, he played football and basketball and successfully hatched a plan for establishing a YMCA in one of the town's unused buildings. He then attended Northwestern University, where he directed award-winning choirs and majored in biology, intending to go to medical school. He matriculated at the Washington University School of Medicine in St. Louis, but sensing that the regimentation of medical school did not suit him, he dropped out after several days.

After service in the military as a medic, he started several businesses. One, a partnership with a college friend, produced disposable hypodermic needles. Eventually, he sold his interest in that business and, with his wife Gayle and one-year-old son, Carl, moved to Bloomington, Indiana.

Having been told by a cousin in the medical profession that catheter-and-wire-based procedures would soon play a pivotal role in medicine, in 1963 Cook started a medical device company in the second bedroom of his family's two-bedroom apartment, where he produced and sold his products. Gayle kept the books and handled quality control.

At a trade show in Chicago, he met a physician from Oregon named Charles Dotter. Dotter, now known as the father of interventional medicine, was one of the first physicians to see the full potential of minimally invasive catheter-based medicine, and he and Cook collaborated to develop many new devices for use in diagnosing and treating diseases. Dotter was featured using Cook-manufactured wires and catheters in a 1964 *Life* magazine article, replete with photos depicting him opening up a narrowed artery in a patient's leg and restoring adequate blood flow, thus enabling the patient to avoid amputation.

Cook's business grew rapidly, morphing over the course of fifty years into a company that today manufactures about sixteen thousand different medical devices. From an initial investment of $1,500, the Cook fortune is now estimated at more than $6 billion.

Strictly in terms of making money, Cook's story is one of remarkable success. But even more remarkable is the fact that, for Cook, the wealth was merely a byproduct of the pursuit of something more important. For men such as Cook and Dotter, money was not the prime motivator for what they did. Dotter, who collaborated with Cook for many years and supplied the ideas for a number of the company's early products, was the first person to whom Cook offered royalty payments. But Dotter refused them—because he cared more about making things happen than about making money. Dotter and Cook were much alike. What really interested both of them was identifying a problem for which they could develop a solution. They loved innovating in ways that would benefit patients.

As their fortune grew, the Cooks manifested a steady indifference to the things money could buy. For many years, Bill drove the same old Pontiac. He and Gayle bought a modest three-bedroom house in 1967, and this remained their primary residence. Cook died in that home in 2011. The Cooks were not interested in making money for the purposes of what the economist Thorsten Veblen famously called "conspicuous consumption." They saw profits as something to be reinvested for the benefit of the business and the community. For them, even philanthropy represented a form of investment.

The Cooks had a special interest in historic preservation. Bill grew up in a small town, and he credited the experience with building his character and making him the person he was. He believed that others deserved to grow up in such communities, and he wanted to do what he could to enrich their civic lives. So he and Gayle devoted much of their giving to preserving and restoring historic buildings in towns and cities across Indiana and neighboring states.

The Cooks' philanthropic philosophy seems to have followed in the footsteps of Andrew Carnegie, the nineteenth-century steel magnate who in 1889 wrote the article "The Gospel of Wealth," in which he suggested that wealthy people should spread their wealth around, as it were, rather than merely hold onto it and then pass it to their children. Perhaps Carnegie's best-known philanthropic endeavor was the funding of Carnegie libraries throughout the United States. More of these libraries were built in Indiana than any other state in the country.

Carnegie would provide a grant to build a library, but only if the people of the community had developed a plan to fund its operations going forward. Like

Carnegie, the Cooks tended to fund projects that showed strong prospects for becoming self-sustaining. One illustrative Cook philanthropic project is the Monroe County YMCA. Cook believed that the people of Bloomington and the surrounding county deserved a larger, better YMCA facility. But a feasibility study conducted by the YMCA national office concluded that a new facility was not warranted. The national representative told Cook and other community leaders that local demand would not support a larger facility, in part because Bloomington is the home of the largest campus of Indiana University, which already provided residents sufficient access to recreational facilities and programs.

When the national office representative finished his presentation, Cook thanked him for his efforts. He then turned to the group and said, "We have heard enough. Now let's get to work building a new YMCA!" Though Cook was no expert on YMCAs, he did know the people of Bloomington, and he also had a vision of the type of facility and programming that they would find attractive. With substantial support from the Cook Group, the YMCA was built, and despite the representative's warnings, it became the largest in Indiana and one of the most successful in the United States.

Perhaps the Cooks' best-known philanthropic project is the historic French Lick–West Baden hotel and resort complex in southern Indiana. In the first decade of the twentieth century, the West Baden Springs Hotel featured the largest free-spanning dome in the world, and it remained the largest in the United States until the 1950s. The area was already a popular tourist destination, thanks to its mineral springs and baths. Accessible by railway, the complex represented an international resort for the well-heeled.

As the Great Depression unfolded, the French Lick–West Baden complex fell on hard times. These were exacerbated by the decline of railroad travel and the rise of the automobile, which made southern states a more attractive tourist destination. Ownership of the properties passed through several hands, with further declines in value each time. By the 1990s the West Baden Springs Hotel was in such a sad state of disrepair that it was closed to the public and the collapse of its dome was considered imminent. The Cooks were asked to provide funding to shore it up. They not only agreed to those funds but also undertook a major restoration effort intended to return the complex to commercial viability. Calculating that gambling would be a necessary factor in the equation, they successfully lobbied lawmakers to authorize it. In 2006, the complex, including a casino, reopened.

Before the renovation, Orange County, Indiana, had one of the state's highest unemployment rates. Since the reopening, unemployment in the area has fallen to among the lowest in the state, and the complex now serves as a training site for students studying hotel and tourism services.

What makes Cook's perspective on service particularly remarkable is the fact that the greater part of it has been expressed through the domain of commerce, by for-profit companies. From the earliest days, working for Cook meant not merely meeting the stipulations of a job description and earning a wage, but also becoming part of a culture with a special set of commitments and aspirations. Though powerfully shaped by its founder, this culture did not force everyone to be just like Bill Cook. It did, however, represent a culture of service that enabled many people to come more fully to life.

One key feature of Cook's culture was a commitment to improving the lives of others. When it came to managing the company, Cook relied less on systems, policies, and procedures than on curiosity, creativity, and initiative. His most important criteria for hiring people included whether he felt job candidates would live up to their word, function as self-starters, get along well with others, and avoid sowing seeds of dissension.

Once Cook satisfied himself that people genuinely enjoyed their work, sought out opportunities to achieve goals, cared about doing the job right and on time, and shared his overall outlook on what makes organizations thrive, he typically gave them free rein to do their work as they saw fit. Job descriptions and organizational charts were less important than the human beings doing the work. If the company had the right people playing key roles, micromanagement was not only unnecessary but counterproductive.

This attitude contrasts sharply with many of Cook's competitors, who typically relied to a much greater extent on constructing the right kind of "system," one in which the job, the means of doing it, and the criteria for assessing it were so clearly spelled out that there was often very little room for individuals to express or develop themselves.

At the Cook Group, people did not feel like interchangeable cogs in a machine. Expectations for performance were high, but individual initiative and judgment played a major role in shaping how those expectations were met. This respect for each person's distinctive capabilities permeated all levels of the organization. Even at the level of production workers, the emphasis at Cook was always on handcraft, not automation. Handcraft offers key benefits. One is the ability to customize products to meet the needs of individual customers. Another is the fact that workers—in contrast to robots—understand what they are making, which opens the door to innovation at the level of the producer. Finally, there is pride in work. At Cook, employees don't just maintain machines; they function as artisans who can say with pride, "I made that."

Another key feature of the Cook culture was egalitarianism. Cook did not pay equal wages across all levels of the organization, but he did want people to be treated fairly and with equal respect. There was no executive dining room; everyone ate in the same cafeteria. People standing in the cafeteria line might turn around and find behind them Bill Cook carrying his own tray and utensils. Time allocated to vacation was the same across the organization, and so was the profit-sharing plan, in which every employee received the same percentage bonus, paid monthly. Cook wanted everyone to feel a part of the same team, from the company president to the people who swept the floors on the nightshift. He was often the first person to arrive in the morning, greeting the night staff by name, asking them about their families, and making the coffee.

Cook managed by walking around, making time to talk to employees, and he encouraged others to do the same. He frequently visited the production floor, asking questions about the work and how it could be improved. Everyone knew that he knew what he was talking about, because the company's entire production staff had once consisted of Bill Cook.

One day an engineer mentioned a new product that was under consideration. "It shows real promise in helping patients," he said, "but we recommend holding off on further development." Cook asked why, and the engineer responded, "Our initial analysis suggests that the profit margins just aren't there." Cook's response was characteristic: "What you just said—I don't want to hear that again. If the device will benefit patients, we should move ahead with it. We can always figure out later how to make the finances work."

Cook's accountant told me that he operated the business for decades without a budget. He did not look at balance sheets. Instead, he wanted to know whether a new idea could make a difference for patients. If so, he wanted to move forward with it. What really made him happy was not counting the dollars but seeing a new product in the hand of a physician who was helping a patient with it. Money was important only to the extent that it kept the lights on.

In addition to serving and enhancing the lives of others through his business, Cook created opportunities for others to do the same. This is a hallmark of truly generous people: They do not feel the need to seize all opportunities for generosity themselves. A single-generation giver meets the needs of others by sharing food, clothing, shelter, and so on, but multigenerational givers encourage their recipients to become givers in their own right, with the hope that many of their recipients will again do the same in turn. This spirit is exemplified in the stories of several Cook employees.

The first person Cook hired was Tom Osborne, the son of a local jeweler. A high school senior expecting to be drafted into the military, Osborne was seeking a summer job. Cook, who had learned some key manufacturing techniques from the senior Osborne, hired the young man, who showed up for work each day at the Cooks' two-bedroom apartment. Despite lacking a college degree, Osborne grew and developed in the role, tackling one engineering challenge after another, eventually becoming the holder of hundreds of US patents.

Cook did not focus on people's academic backgrounds or professional qualifications. He did not particularly care what schools prospective employees had attended, their class rank or academic honors. What mattered to Cook was whether a fire burned in their bellies—an eagerness to do something, to make a difference. And when he found such people, as in the case of Osborne, he gave them all the responsibility they could handle, inviting them to spread their wings and soar as high as they could.

Phyllis McCullough's story is similar. She grew up in a working-class family and had no formal education beyond high school. She came to work for Cook as a receptionist, answering the phone, greeting people who came through the front door, and taking dictation. But like Osborne, McCullough paid attention to what was going on and soon began offering suggestions about how the business could run more effectively. After all, she knew Cook's employees—the people of Bloomington—and she was able to see the company and its mission from their points of view.

McCullough's perspectives helped to build not only particular policies, but a whole culture that defined the company. For instance, she worked with Cook to develop the company's innovative profit-sharing program. Eventually, she rose to serve as president of the company for more than a decade.

Kem Hawkins was a music teacher at a local high school, where he also directed the band. Cook always enjoyed music, and he admired the way Hawkins handled the students. The Cooks attended a recital at which they witnessed Hawkins' ability to find something to praise in every student's performance, no matter how poor it was. One student's piece proved particularly ear splitting, but Hawkins told the young man that he admired how, when his turn came, he resolutely picked up his instrument and his music and strode confidently to the front of the room.

Hawkins had no experience with medicine, biological science, or medical devices, but he clearly operated with a deep understanding of people and a genuine commitment to excellence—exactly what Cook was looking for in a leader. Hawkins eventually succeeded McCullough as president, where he helped to promote the company culture that made the good of the patient the ultimate standard of whether the company was on the right track. He encouraged everyone "to do the right thing for the right reason all the time."

The stories of Osborne, McCullough, and Hawkins show how generosity can work through commerce. Cook challenged people and expected them to work hard. They knew they were responsible for getting results. Yet he also gave people considerable independence and autonomy. Instead of barking out orders, he asked for their help. What Cook provided was not a rigid set of policies and procedures that had to be followed to the letter, but a challenge and an opportunity, which proved liberating for those who rose to it.

Cook regarded it as axiomatic that the company should never put its employees or their families at risk. If the company faced a choice between increasing profits and protecting employees, its culture called for accepting a lower level of profit. As a result, the Cook Group has never had a layoff in its first fifty years of existence. Unlike most of its competitors, who produce the vast majority of their products overseas, Cook still produces 80 percent of its products domestically. And when a Cook-funded basketball facility called Cook Hall opened at Indiana University, the commemorative plaque bore the name of every Cook employee.

The terms "philanthropy," "giving," "sharing," and "generosity" were all used long before the US tax code attempted to draw a distinction between for-profit and nonprofit corporations. While many constituencies have large interests in maintaining this distinction and the tax breaks that accompany nonprofit status, we need to be careful to avoid allowing something as byzantine as the tax code to dictate our understanding of generosity. Generosity thrives on insight and creativity, and these attributes are not confined to organizations that eschew the marketplace.

In Bill Cook's mind, the Cook company existed to make a difference for patients, its employees, and the communities in which it was based. Its purpose was not to extract value from patients, employees, and communities that Bill Cook could then use to buy expensive homes and automobiles. Its purpose was to serve those patients, employees, and communities, to play a role in helping to make their lives better. If the company did that well, it would prosper, but the economic returns were always regarded as the byproduct of the pursuit of something more important. Those returns provided a way of determining whether the company was on the right track, but they were not its primary goal.

In some cases, the profit motive spawns corruption. There is no guarantee that just because a business is making money, it is serving the public good. A variety of criminal activities, such as extortion, drug dealing, child prostitution, and murder for hire, are clearly toxic. Many others types of business are largely indifferent as regards human welfare—large swathes of the entertainment industry, for example. But other companies exist for the explicit purpose of enriching human life.

When a company the likes of the Cook Group develops a new product that enables physicians to diagnose and treat diseases with lower cost, less risk, and greater benefit, it is clearly benefiting patients and those who care for them. When it provides safe and secure employment for thousands of people, it is enriching their lives, in part because it gives them an opportunity to know that they are making a real difference. And when it provides its employees with an opportunity not merely to be gainfully employed but to grow and develop as human beings, it is providing an extra measure of enrichment.

There is a difference between knowing that we did our job and knowing that the job we did made a difference. Most importantly, there is a difference between knowing that we did a job that made a difference and knowing that we expanded, enriched, and redefined the job we did, becoming different and better people and helping to create a different and better organization and community in the process. This is the kind of work Bill Cook sought to provide.

nine

EBENEZER
The Spirit of Service

TO PERSUADE OTHERS TO SHARE THEIR TIME, TALENT, OR TREASURE, several alternatives present themselves. One is to hold a gun to their head and threaten to pull the trigger if they do not hand it over. But this, of course, is not generosity, but robbery. The fact that the people with the guns do not profit personally—that they are functioning as latter-day Robin Hoods—provides no excuse.

Another alternative is to threaten potential givers with civil and even criminal sanctions, including fines and imprisonment. This, however, is also not generosity, but taxation. Where genuine generosity is concerned, the fact that the revenues are part of a legislated social welfare program adds no moral luster to the act, and the moral excellence of generosity is not realized merely by paying taxes in a social welfare state.

It is also possible to entice potential givers with various kinds of awards, or even financial incentives. Once again, this is not generosity, but commerce. People who give in order to get something for themselves are not really giving but engaging in a transaction.

As the excellence of generosity cannot be compelled, it cannot be accidental either. It is a weak form of generosity if I leave $20 on the table top and someone else happens to pick it up, even if that person is in a state of dire need. To be sure, we need not always know the particular person or people we are helping. For example, we may not know the names and faces of the future recipients of a scholarship fund we establish. Yet we need a clear idea of what recipients need, such as food, housing, or education, and how the opportunity we are providing will enrich their lives.

Generosity, like every other human excellence, must be voluntary. We must know what we are doing, and we must choose it for the sake of the person or people we are endeavoring to aid. Generous acts must flow from a sincere interest in the welfare of others and a desire to enrich their lives.

It is equally important that such acts arise from a charitable character. Every act of generosity is good in itself, but it is especially admirable when it flows directly from the charitable disposition of the giver. A day in which we have acted generously but once is more worthy than a day in which we have not acted generously at all.

Generosity is about more than transferring resources from one person to another. It is about bringing to full fruition the human potential for excellence. Even an unskilled performer may occasionally strike the ball or the note soundly, but the real beauty lies in striking well on a consistent basis, because only then do we really know what we are doing. The moral life is as much about being as doing. Good people wish less to act charitably, in the sense of acting as if they were charitable, than to express truly charitable character through action. There is a sense in which we learn to be charitable by acting charitably, but our ultimate goal is not to pretend, but to truly be.

Aptitudes, temperaments, and interests differ from person to person. Some have a leg up on others when it comes to the degree to which they are naturally disposed to generosity. Yet generosity is not purely natural, and it can be powerfully influenced by the manner in which we are reared, educated, and habituated. If our parents delight in generosity, there is a greater chance that our own charitable inclinations will be developed and expressed.

The same is true if we receive an education that helps us understand the nature of generosity and the important difference that charitable acts can make in the lives of recipients and givers. Emulation can make a big difference. If our friends are charitable and devote themselves to charitable works, then we are more likely to do so ourselves.

Generosity is an important ingredient in the recipe for a full human life. It is only when we have become genuinely charitable that we fully understand what we have to contribute. People who exhibit no interest in generosity, and who are not engaged in fostering it, are missing an important element in life. They may be oblivious to the needs of others, or they may suppose that life is all about accumulating for the self. They may even be rich.

But the moral dimension of an ungenerous life is necessarily impoverished. The inability to part with what we have and to share our best with others represents a moral failing. We may coerce, threaten, or even bribe people to give, but when it comes to genuine generosity, education and persuasion are the only means available. We neglect the topic of educating people to be generous at our own considerable peril.

How can we educate for generosity? How can we help those we care most about, including our children and grandchildren, realize their full charitable potential? To begin with, we might ask them to participate in charitable works. We might encourage them to keep company with charitable people. We might even invite them to read philosophical, theological, and literary works that explore generosity. Some of these works might include biographies and novels depicting generosity in action and at its best. Among such works we might include the Gospel of Luke, Shakespeare's *Tempest*, and Dostoevsky's *The Brothers Karamazov*. Such works offer not only insight, but inspiration.

In the interest of understanding the vice as well as the virtue associated with generosity, we might also choose works that show generosity at its worst, through portraits of misers and misanthropes, as revealed in the works of Machiavelli, Jonathan Swift, and Molière. We might also explore the human ascent from the pit of avarice to the heights of generosity. Such a transformation is beautifully portrayed in one of the best-known myths of modern times, Charles Dickens's *A Christmas Carol*.

Charles Dickens

Charles Dickens (1812–1870) was the second of eight children of a naval pay clerk who provided his son with a few years of formal schooling. His father lived beyond his means, however, and his spendthrift ways soon landed him in debtor's prison. The boy's education ceased and he was forced to work long days in a boot black factory. This experience shaped Dickens's lifelong interest in the working and living conditions of the poor.

As a young man, Dickens found work in a law office, followed by a stint as a freelance reporter and then a journalist reporting on Parliament and election campaigns. This work led to his first literary collection, *Sketches by Boz*, which was published in 1836 and brought him into a circle of friends and associates that included important literary figures. Dickens's next major work, *The Pickwick Papers*, began to make him famous.

Dickens then began producing his most famous novels. Between 1839 and 1861 he published *Oliver Twist, A Christmas Carol, David Copperfield, Bleak House, Hard Times, Little Dorrit, A Tale of Two Cities,* and *Great Expectations*. By the time he died, he had written more than fifteen novels and hundreds of short stories and nonfiction articles.

The personal dimension of Dickens's adult life was often difficult. He married a journalist's daughter, Catherine Hogarth, who bore him ten children. Eventually, Dickens left her, saying that they had been unhappy for many years, but he also had fallen in love with an actress, Ellen Ternan, who was eighteen years old, the same age as Dickens's youngest daughter. He was also a less-than-exemplary father, sending his sons away as teenagers.

Despite whiffs of scandal during his lifetime, no writer working in English had ever been as popular as Dickens, and many of the characters he created—such as Samuel Pickwick, Ebenezer Scrooge, Oliver Twist, and David Copperfield—are among the best known in world literature.

Dickens is credited with introducing the serial publication of works of fiction, which allowed him to take readers' reactions into account as he wrote. Many of his characters were drawn from his own life. For example, *David Copperfield* is often read as a thinly veiled autobiographical account. In addition to his literary output, Dickens was also a dedicated critic of poverty, an advocate for social reform, and a fierce promoter of the rights of children.

A Christmas Carol

First published in 1843, Dickens's novella *A Christmas Carol* tells the tale of businessman Ebenezer Scrooge, a man who represents the antithesis of generosity. In the person of Scrooge, we behold the meanness, pettiness, and ultimate absurdity of the hoarder's life. We also witness his transformation from a misanthrope into a truly charitable human being. As events unfold, Scrooge ceases regarding other people as threats to be defended against or idiots whose needs and appetites can be exploited for personal gain. Instead, he discovers through them opportunities to give and to make the most of what he has to contribute.

We first meet Scrooge on Christmas Eve, the anniversary of the death of his business partner and moral alter ego Jacob Marley, for whom Scrooge served as both the sole mourner and sole residual legatee. Scrooge is described as a "scraping, clutching, covetous old sinner," "hard and sharp as flint, from which no steel had ever struck out generous fire." His path in life has been a solitary one, with no interest in or sympathy for others. When his nephew, Fred, visits Scrooge's office and, moved by the spirit of Christmas, invites him to be his guest for the holiday, Scrooge remarks that the younger man can have nothing to celebrate, for he is short of money. Fred replies that Christmas is a time when men and women recognize their shared humanity and "open up their shut-up hearts freely." Scrooge is unmoved. Seeing no profit in it, he would prefer to spend the day alone.

Then Scrooge is visited by two charity workers, who ask him to contribute to a collection for the poor and destitute. Scrooge asks whether the prisons and workhouses are still in operation. Assured that they are, he responds that he intends to contribute nothing. "I help support the establishments I have mentioned," he says, and points out that they "cost enough." The charity workers reply that many would rather die than go to a prison or workhouse, to which Scrooge replies, "If they would rather die, they had better do it, and decrease the surplus population." The misfortunes of others do not concern Scrooge. "It is enough for a man to understand his own business, and not to interfere with other people's," he says.

Scrooge then turns to his threadbare clerk, Bob Cratchit, who is scarcely able to support his large family with his meager salary. Scrooge resents that Cratchit expects to get Christmas day off with pay. The idea that anyone would give away something for nothing is not only highly objectionable, but essentially incomprehensible to him. From the standpoint of a greedy soul, the giving of gifts of any kind simply makes no sense.

That night, Scrooge is visited by the ghost of his dead partner. Marley drags heavy chains made of cash-boxes, keys, padlocks, ledgers, deeds, and heavy purses. "I wear the chain I forged in life," cries the ghost, a chain not so different from the one that Scrooge is forging for himself. The ghost describes his existence as an "incessant torture of remorse," yet "no space of regret can make amends for one's life's opportunity misused."

Scrooge is perplexed. "But you were always such a good man of business, Jacob," he offers. The ghost thunders his reply: "Business! Mankind was my business! The common welfare was my business: charity, mercy, forbearance, and benevolence were all my business." The ghost is hinting at a new model of busyness, one that subordinates the making of a living to the making of a life. His model is less transactional than transformational, measured not by what people accumulate, but by what they contribute.

Marley's ghost warns Scrooge that he has a chance of escaping his former partner's bitter fate. Scrooge will be visited by three spirits, without whom he has no hope of avoiding the path the ghost of his partner now treads. As the ghost exits through the window, Scrooge's eyes are drawn outward, where he sees the air filled with phantoms, all bound by chains. The narrator notes, "The misery with them all was, clearly, that they sought to interfere, for good, in human matters, but had lost the power forever."

The visit of Marley's ghost plants the seeds of Scrooge's transformation, but the visits of each of the three spirits effect it. The Ghost of Christmas Past, the Ghost of Christmas Present, and the Ghost of Christmas Yet to Come challenge Scrooge to see his life and the lives of others from a new perspective. They do not bombard Scrooge with commands or threaten him with punishments. Instead, they simply enable him to see what his life once was, what it has become, and where its trajectory will lead. In other words, they enable him to look at his life anew, with a long sense of time. These new vantage points prove morally transformative.

To fully understand our earthly affairs, the story implies, we must view our lives from a spiritual perspective. Viewed from a purely worldly point of view, no transformation is possible. Through the good graces of the three spirits, Scrooge is afforded the opportunity to read his own biography, to see his life story retold in a single night. Only the spiritual perspective enables Scrooge to appreciate changes so gradual that otherwise they would be imperceptible. He must see from a larger perspective—not day to day, but year to year and decade to decade—what he has made of his life. Though the moving finger has writ and moved on, there is still hope for Scrooge; he can still choose a different path. So, too, perhaps, can we.

The Past

When the Ghost of Christmas Past arrives, the terrified Scrooge finds himself quaking in bed, "face to face with the unearthly visitor," who, the narrator says, is "as close as I am now to you, and I am standing in the spirit at your elbow." As Scrooge is being visited by spirits, the narrator implies, so, too, spirits are drawing close to each of us. As Scrooge will be made to follow Socrates's injunction and examine his own life, so we, by accompanying Scrooge and the spirits, will be pressed to reexamine our own.

The Spirit reaches out to Scrooge and leads him to the window. Scrooge protests, "I am mortal, and liable to fall." Scrooge fears for his safety, but in fact, he has been exposed all his life to a quite different sort of fall. This is not a physical fall that might send him crashing to the ground, but a moral fall that has been happening for many years. It is not the sort of fall that breaks the ankle or the elbow, but the kind that breaks the spirit. To know what he has lost, and to realize that the loss has been of his own making, Scrooge must witness it firsthand, through a kind of time-lapse photography.

The Spirit first takes Scrooge to his old school, where he sees happy boys wishing each other a merry Christmas. But one solitary child remains in the school, neglected by his friends. Scrooge begins to weep. "I wish . . . ," he says, "but it is too late now."

"What is the matter?" asks the Spirit.

"Nothing," says Scrooge. "There was a boy singing a Christmas carol at my door last night. I should like to have given him something: that's all."

Then Scrooge sees himself grown older, again alone. A little girl, his sister, bursts into the room and announces that she has come to fetch him. Scrooge is to come home for good, for his father has grown "much kinder than he used to be." What do people long for at Christmas? Home. Scrooge's father has changed, and changed in such a way that he now wants his son home for Christmas. Perhaps Ebenezer is not the first Scrooge to receive a spiritual visitation?

Beholding the scene with his sister, Scrooge is reminded of what a delicate creature she had always been, though "she had a large heart." The Spirit adds, "She died a woman, and had, as I think, children." "One child," Scrooge corrects—Fred, his nephew. Some people's hearts continue beating for many a year, and those of others cease before their time.

The great heart and spirit of Scrooge's sister lives on in her only son—the very nephew whose kind-hearted invitation to celebrate the holidays together Scrooge had so meanly rebuffed that very same day. We are invited to glimpse what Scrooge has missed—that his nephew carries on his mother's generosity and that his entreaties, like his mother's, are summoning Ebenezer home to the true spirit of Christmas.

Next they visit the site of the young Scrooge's apprenticeship and the home of his old boss, Fezziwig. It is Christmas Eve, and Fezziwig insists that everyone cease working and gather at his home to celebrate the holiday with a banquet of plenty and merry dances. As the evening draws to a close, the Spirit turns to Scrooge and remarks, "A small matter to make these silly folks so full of gratitude." The Spirit urges Scrooge to listen as two apprentices praise their boss. Then the Spirit adds, "He has spent but a few pounds of your mortal money: three or four perhaps. Is that so much that he deserves this praise?"

Scrooge leaps to his former master's defense: "The happiness he gives is quite as great as if it cost a fortune." The Spirit inquires why Scrooge looks troubled. "I should like to be able to say a word or two to my clerk just now. That's all."

It seems that we cannot evaluate the worth of a party, or for that matter any gift, by the amount of money spent on it. The Fezziwigs are sharing something nonfungible, yet even Scrooge recognizes it as quite valuable. They are enriching their guests' spirits, not their purses, and showing them the true meaning of holiday festivity.

Next we see Scrooge still older, and noticeably changed. There is now an "eager, greedy, restless motion in his eye, which shows the passion that had taken root, and where the shadow of the growing tree would fall." This Scrooge is speaking with a fair young woman, his betrothed. It becomes apparent that she is releasing him from a pledge of marriage. He protests that he does not wish to be released, but she persists. "You fear the world too much," she says. "I have seen your nobler aspirations fall off one by one, until the master passion, gain, engrosses you." She continues, "If you were free, can even I believe that you would choose a dowerless girl—you who, in your very confidence with her, weigh everything by gain?"

Then Scrooge sees her grown into a woman and mother, tenderly presiding over her own young children who play and laugh with her. Her husband arrives, and the children pick their father's pockets for the presents he has brought them. Later, the younger children off to bed, he sits by the fireside with his wife and daughter. Beholding this scene, Scrooge marvels that the young girl "might have called him father, and been a spring-time in the haggard winter of his life." At this, "his sight grew very dim indeed."

Then the husband reports to his wife that he has seen an old friend of hers that very afternoon. "Who?" she asks. "Why, Mr. Scrooge," he responds. "I passed his office window; and as it was not shut up, and he had a candle inside, I could scarcely help seeing him. His partner lies upon the point of death, I hear; and there he sat alone. Quite alone in the world, I do believe." Scrooge begs the Spirit to take him away, saying, "I cannot bear it." The Ghost of Christmas Past leaves him.

Scrooge is indeed alone. He sees as he has never seen before that his habit of treating everyone and everything in terms of personal gain has rendered him isolated and loveless. He has no one else. Seeking to protect himself from a hazardous world by amassing wealth, he has landed himself not in a fortress but a prison, one of his own making. And he is this prison's sole inmate—condemned, it seems, to serve out his life sentence in solitary confinement.

The Present

Scrooge is visited next by the Ghost of Christmas Present, who takes him on a tour of London on Christmas morning. The city is transformed and full of delights— shops and stores overflowing with delicious treats. Then church bells issue the call to worship, and the streets fill with people decked out in their finest clothes, their faces shining gaily.

They soon come to the house of Scrooge's clerk, Bob Cratchit. Scrooge is amazed when the Spirit blesses it: "Bob had but fifteen bob a-week himself; he pocketed on Saturdays but fifteen copies of his Christian name; and yet the Ghost of Christmas Present blessed his four-roomed house." In manifesting his generous and hearty nature, the Spirit is not seeking out the financially astute or the rich. Quite the opposite, he seems to display a special sympathy for the poor and downtrodden.

The Spirit and Scrooge enter the Cratchit's humble abode and observe. Mrs. Cratchit is "dressed out but poorly in a twice-turned gown, but brave in ribbons, which are cheap and make a goodly show for sixpence." The older children are helping to prepare Christmas dinner, while the younger ones tear about with anticipation. Then Bob himself arrives with Tiny Tim, their youngest son, who "bore a little crutch, and had his limbs supported by an iron frame."

Bob relates that on their way home, Tiny Tim confided in him that he hoped people in church had seen him, "because he was a cripple, and it might be pleasant to them to remember upon Christmas Day, who made lame beggars walk, and blind men see." In relating this story, Bob's voice trembles, but he maintains that Tiny Tim is "growing strong and hearty."

The family sit at the table and share a modest feast. Then Mrs. Cratchit fetches the pudding, and everybody has words of praise, "but nobody said or thought that it was at all a small pudding for such a large family." The Cratchits lead lives of scarcity, but they celebrate the holiday in a spirit of abundance and gratitude. Scrooge, by contrast, possesses in abundance, yet is so tortured by the desire for more that he is unable to celebrate at all.

"God bless us every one," says Tiny Tim, in his weak voice.

"Spirit," says Scrooge, with an interest he had never felt before. "Tell me if Tiny Tim will live."

"I see a vacant seat in the poor chimney-corner," replies the Spirit, "and a crutch without an owner, carefully preserved. If these shadows remain unaltered by the Future, the child will die."

"Oh, no, kind Spirit," says Scrooge, "say he will be spared."

The Spirit repeats, "If these shadows remain unaltered by the Future, none other of my race . . . will find him here." And then the Spirit adds, in words dripping with irony in Scrooge's ears, "What then. If he be like to die, he had better do it, and decrease the surplus population."

This calls to mind a terrible observation once attributed to Joseph Stalin: "The death of one man is a tragedy, but the death of millions is a statistic." As long as Scrooge sees the poor in the abstract, their lives and deaths mean less to him than the financial figures that fill his ledger books. On beholding a real family and a real child, though, his view of the matter is quite transformed. There is a big difference between poverty in the abstract and a poor human being, and those who seek to educate for service need to be mindful of this distinction.

The Spirit continues: "Man, if man you be in heart, forbear that wicked cant until you have discovered What the surplus is, and Where it is. . . . It may be that in the sight of Heaven, you are more worthless and less fit to live than millions like this poor man's child." Scrooge is stunned to silence.

He sees that the Cratchits are not a "handsome family." They do not dress well, and they own little. Yet they are "happy, grateful, pleased with one another, and contented with the time." As they fade behind the Spirit's torch, Scrooge "had his eye upon them, and especially on Tiny Tim, until the last."

Scrooge has discovered something about the Cratchits that he never suspected. First, he has discovered that they have a life. They are not merely "the poor," but flesh-and-blood human beings, each endowed with a distinctive personality and character, each bearing a set of life aspirations. Not only are they real, but in crucial respects they are more real than Scrooge, whose cramped existence exhibits few signs of real life. As the Spirit implies, there is some doubt about Scrooge's humanity. Our humanity is not in all respects given to us. In some respects, it is an achievement, and we must earn it, and re-earn it, every day of our lives.

Next the Spirit takes Scrooge across the land, to a place where miners live, then to a lonely lighthouse, then to a ship's crew far out at sea. In every case, despite their hard lives, each person has "a kinder word for another on that day than on any other day of the year; and had shared to some extent in its festivities; and had remembered those he cared for at a distance, and had known that they delighted to remember him." By comparison, Scrooge has no one to remember, and no one is remembering him.

Scrooge begins to realize that such remembering is all. When disaster falls, property can be replaced. But memories of the kind contained in family photo albums are irreplaceable. They are priceless, and no one's memories, whether rich or poor, are any more or less precious than anyone else's. In this respect, all human beings are equal, and each equally dear to God.

Then the Spirit takes Scrooge to a festive holiday party at Fred's house. The conversation touches on Scrooge, and though some guests disparage him, Fred leaps to his defense, calling him a "comical old fellow." Though admittedly his uncle isn't pleasant, Fred wishes him nothing ill, for "his offences carry their own punishment. . . . he loses some pleasant moments, which could do him no harm. I am sure he loses pleasanter companions than he can find in his own thoughts, either in his mouldy old office, or his dusty chambers." Yet, Fred continues, "I mean to give him the same chance every year, whether he likes it or not, for I pity him."

Later the partygoers play a guessing game, in which everyone tries to guess what one of their company is thinking of. Fred thinks of "an animal, a live animal, rather a disagreeable animal, a savage animal, an animal that grunted and growled sometimes, and talked sometimes, and lived in London." They guess a bull, a tiger, a bear. With each incorrect guess, the nephew bursts out in a fresh roar of laughter. At last, one of the sisters discovers the solution. "It's your uncle Scrooge!"

Scrooge, who would have preferred to be feared instead of liked, discovers that his greed has made him a laughing stock. He is not respected for his financial good sense; instead, he is despised as an absurdity. In tending strictly to his own business, he has made himself pathetic. As he has busied himself filling his coffers with coin, his humanity has been depleted.

Finally the Spirit leads Scrooge out to the almshouses, hospitals, and jails, "every misery's refuge." At each stop, if "vain man" has not barred the Spirit from entry, he leaves his blessing.

Finally, the night is done, and the Spirit begins to fade. But Scrooge is disturbed by something strange he sees beneath the Spirit's robe—something like a foot or a claw. Then from the folds of his robe emerge two children, "wretched, abject, frightful, hideous, miserable."

Scrooge draws back, appalled. "Spirit, are they yours?" he asks.

"They are Man's," corrects the Spirit. "This boy is Ignorance. This girl is Want. Beware them both, and all of their degree, but most of all beware this boy, for on his brow I see that written which is Doom."

"Have they no refuge or resource?" cries Scrooge.

The Spirit turns on him with biting words. "Are there no prisons? Are they no workhouses?"

At this moment, the clock strikes twelve, and the Spirit is gone. The worst distortion of human nature is not Tiny Tim's withered limbs. It is the grotesque spectacle of unloved and unnurtured children, souls warped by ignorance and want. Scrooge has lived most of his life devoid of understanding, failing to recognize—let alone to attend to—the most urgent human business. Now he is getting an education. Now he is being confronted with the narrowness and superficiality of his own heart.

Yet to Come

The third Spirit, the Ghost of Christmas Yet to Come, is draped in black, foreboding, and utterly silent. Scrooge says that he fears this specter more than any he has seen, "but I know your purpose is to do me good, and as I hope to live to be another man from what I was, I am prepared to bear you company, and do it with a thankful heart." Far from wishing the visitations were over, Scrooge now declares that time with the Spirit is precious to him, and urges the Spirit to move quickly.

They travel to the city, where men are discussing a funeral. None of those present knows of anyone who plans to attend, but one offers to do so if a meal is provided. Next the Spirit and Scrooge go to Scrooge's office, but he is not there. Scrooge surmises that in the future he has indeed implemented the change in his life he has been resolving to make.

Next they go to a particularly infamous part of the city, where two women and a man arrive with bundles to present to a second man. It becomes apparent that they stole their items from a dead man. They tell each other that doing so is no cause for blame since, "Who's the worse for the loss of a few things like these? Not a dead man, I suppose." After all, you can't take it with you, and these vultures are only attempting to make the most for themselves of what the dead man left behind.

The assembled surmise that the deceased must have been a "wicked old screw," since he had no one "to look after him when he was struck with Death, instead of lying gasping out his last there, alone by himself." As they exchange their ill-gotten gains for coins, they laugh. "He frightened everyone away from him when he was alive, to profit us when he was dead." The narrator notes that death is able to dress the greedy with terrors, but of the "loved, revered, and honoured head," death cannot "make one feature odious."

It is as though death magnifies the features that most characterized the life. After a twisted life ends, it becomes uglier still, but the nobility of the good shines on after a good life has passed away. Though the hand in death may be cold and the heart stilled, the hand in life was "open, generous, and true," and the heart was "brave, warm, and tender." People who live only for themselves die completely, but those who have lived for others and made a difference in others' lives do not vanish completely—their "good deeds . . . sow the world with life immortal!"

The Spirit then takes Scrooge back to the Cratchit home. The oldest boy is reading from a book: "And he took a child, and set him in the midst of them." As he utters these words, Mrs. Cratchit covers her eyes with her hands. Bob is not home yet, and she remarks that he has been walking more slowly of late.

At last Bob arrives, and the two youngest children climb up on his knees, begging their father not to be grieved. It becomes apparent that he has just been visiting Tiny Tim's grave. Later he tells his family, "I know that when we recollect how patient and how mild he was, although he was a little, little child, we shall not quarrel easily among ourselves, nor forget Tiny Tim in doing it." Though he has died, Tiny Tim lives on in the hearts of his family, above all that of his father. His gentle, frail spirit continues to shine like a beacon of goodness in their lives.

The deaths of the greedy man and Tiny Tim present a remarkable contrast. The former brings out the worst in people. No one mourns him or pays his memory even a modicum of respect. Instead, jokes are made at his expense. His death represents nothing more than an opportunity for self-enrichment. By contrast, the death of Tiny Tim brings out the best in everyone.

In life, Tiny Tim wanted others to see him so that they might be reminded of one who healed. In death, he memorializes the dignity of the meek, the mild, the weak, and the wounded. The greedy man accumulated a great deal in life, but in death he left behind nothing but a few rags. By contrast, Tiny Tim was small and frail in life, but his memory brings goodness and happiness to life. The man of greed had grown to fear and hate every moment of his life, but Tiny Tim had developed the excellence of trust.

The Spirit next takes Scrooge to a graveyard. Scrooge begs the Spirit to tell him whether what he has seen are shades of what *will* be, or shadows of things that merely *may* be. But the Spirit only points to a neglected grave. Scrooge persists: "Men's courses foreshadow certain ends, to which, if persevered in, they must lead. But if the courses be departed from, the ends will change. Say it is thus with what you show me." But the Spirit remains silent and immovable.

Scrooge creeps up to the grave, trembling as he advances. On the headstone he reads what he had most feared: "Ebenezer Scrooge." "Spirit," he pleads, "I am not the man I was. I will not be the man I must have been but for this intercourse." Scrooge begs again that he may change these shadows. "I will honour Christmas in my heart," he vows, "and try to keep it all the year. I will live in the Past, the Present, and the Future. The Spirits of all Three shall strive within me." Then he awakens back in his own room on Christmas morning. He is a transformed person, sending a large turkey to the Cratchit family, spending the day in celebration with his nephew and his wife, giving Bob a raise, and becoming like a second father to Tiny Tim.

Transformation

Scrooge is grateful for what the Spirits have shown him, but why? After all, they have revealed him to be a petty, self-centered, greedy old man who is feared, despised, and laughed at by many and admired and loved by none.

Though the visage they reveal is an ugly and regrettable one, Scrooge is grateful because the Spirits have shown him the truth about himself. Only in knowing himself does he stand a chance of changing his course and becoming a better man. The Spirits have made this possible by showing Scrooge who he is, but also by showing him who he had been and who he will be if he does not change. Only when he sees his life in this broader temporal perspective is he able to grasp its true significance, to size up his life and see what he is amounting to.

The Spirits show Scrooge his life's silhouette, cast against the lives of those who know him. When he sees what his life could have contributed and could still contribute, he sees it as if for the first time.

What Scrooge has needed is not a lesson in the importance of tangible things. After all, he had put all his faith in tangible things. What he needed was a lesson about intangible things. Life without tangible things may be difficult and even impossible. But merely supplying such needs, even in abundance, does not guarantee a rich life. In fact, inappropriately coveting such goods all but excludes that possibility.

We cannot get even the lower things right unless we first become appropriately oriented toward the higher things. By ignoring and even disparaging the very notion of anything higher than personal gain, Scrooge sentenced himself to a mean life.

He is redeemed when the Spirits give him the opportunity to see what he has been missing—the possibility for compassion, forgiveness, and love. Since such excellences are immaterial, insights into them are best delivered through spiritual media. The Spirits show Scrooge that the goods of the heart are every bit as real as the goods of the strongbox. They show him that, by recognizing a part of himself that he had forgotten, and by realizing that he shares it in common with every other human being, his humanity can still be restored. Redemption is still possible. He can still learn generosity. And by viewing our own lives through the lens of Scrooge's story, so can each of us.

Achieving extraordinary ends requires extraordinary means. We need narrative, and not just narrative, but myth. And such myth must reach out to us from beyond the worldly, beckoning us to the realm of the spiritual. It must transport us to a thin place, where the worldly and the heavenly are brought into close proximity.

When imagination brings us to such a place, a new alchemy becomes possible, opening up new possibilities for human character, understanding, and redemption. Only here, in close proximity to the spiritual, is real education for generosity possible. Only here, Dickens suggests, can we learn that service plays a far greater role than acquisition in imbuing our lives with meaning.

ten

VINCENT
Service through Art

SUCCESS AND FAILURE CAN BE SURPRISINGLY DIFFICULT TO DISTINGUISH
from one another. Reflecting on my own life, I can think of times when fears came
to pass or ambitions were thwarted in ways that stung me badly at the time. In the
long run, however, I look back on some of those disappointments with a sense of
thanksgiving.

Asked as a child what I wanted to be when I grew up, I might have replied a
secret agent or a major league baseball player. Now I regard the fact that many
of those dreams never materialized with great relief. Occasionally, the things we
want most are the things we need least. Sometimes, the things we desire least turn
out to be the most important.

How often would our lives and the lives of people around us be impoverished
if our wishes were granted? In weaker moments, we may yearn to strike it rich in
some way, dreaming that we might someday while away our days sipping cocktails
on an exotic beach. But how would losing the need to work affect our prospects
for fully developing as human beings and contributing meaningfully to the lives
of others?

This is one reason why the lives of child prodigies—people who excel remarkably at a young age—often turn out to be unenviable. Shining at a young age can
stunt other dimensions of development. Acquiring wealth too soon may only un-
derwrite the escalating indulgence of immature passions until all passion is spent.

Setbacks can open up unexpected possibilities in life. A prestigious award
goes to someone else. A coveted career path is closed off. A first love turns out
not to be a life partner. Often, it is only when one way forward is blocked that we
become aware of another that leads in an ultimately more fruitful direction.

In retrospect, apparently little things turn out to be big. Someone who knows
someone happens to mention a possibility that turns out to be one of the most significant opportunities we ever encounter. A chance event in a classroom, a workplace, or a park brings us face to face with the love of our life.

At what point on the journey through life can we be certain that we grasp the full range of possibilities and consequences open to us? If not in childhood or adolescence, would it be middle age, or perhaps when we are grandparents? What if we never reach such a point? What if the wiser we get, the more our respect deepens for our limitations?

For those who believe in the power of prayer, this is one problem with what is sometimes called petitionary prayer, that is, requesting divine help in satisfying personal desires. Do we really want—let alone know—what is truly most appropriate? Perhaps there are purposes at work in reality that far exceed our ability to perceive, let alone direct. An alternative to praying for help that "my will be done" is the prayer that requests "thy will be done."

Most of us experience frustration from time to time as our desires are thwarted. But what if the most notable constraint many of us face is not the limited ability to make our dreams a reality but the limited nature of our dreams? Who among us has not at one time or another put our own desires ahead of everyone and everything else?

Our greatest limitation turns out to be our own imagination.

Consider one of the great stories of failure in recent centuries. I have in mind an individual who failed at two careers, whose two proposals of marriage were both rejected, who remained dependent on his family for financial support virtually his entire life, and whose unkempt appearance testified to his abject poverty. He suffered from several chronic illnesses. He invariably struck those who met him as eccentric and moody. His life was marked by frequent bouts of despair. He died decades prematurely and nearly unknown. An artist, his body of work amounts to more than two thousand paintings, drawings, and sketches, yet he sold only a single work in his lifetime.

I am referring, of course, to Vincent Van Gogh, one of the world's great painters. Vincent's life story can be told as an almost unending succession of failures, culminating in his death—unheralded and penniless at the age of only thirty-seven years. As one commentator has noted, at the time of his death, his work was known to only a few, and it was admired by fewer still.

Vincent's will was repeatedly thwarted to such an extent that he found himself for long stretches of his life gripped by despair. And yet these grave disappointments opened up new possibilities in his life that ultimately left the world a richer and more beautiful place. We can only hope that these many disappointments seemed to Vincent himself adequate to compensate for the price he had to pay.

Born in 1853 in the Netherlands, Vincent died in France in 1890. He came from a family of clergymen and art dealers, the former including both his father and grandfather, and the latter both his uncle and brother. His brother Theo played a particularly important role in this story, because during an approximately eighteen-year period up to their deaths in the same year, they exchanged hundreds of letters, with more than six hundred of them surviving today.

Vincent clearly experienced a powerful sense of calling throughout much of his life. He once wrote Theo, "Man is not put on this earth merely to be happy, nor even to be simply honest. He is here to realize great things for humanity." Many art historians and biographers have come to see Vincent as a person who pursued two successive callings in life, ultimately abandoning his first calling and turning to the second.

The first calling, as they see it, was Vincent's religious calling, his aspiration to follow his father and grandfather and become a minister. Before he turned in his late twenties to his second calling, as an artist, such scholars maintain that Vincent first had to completely renounce his first, turning his back on the ministry and perhaps on religion generally.

In fact, however, the real story appears to be both more complex and more illuminating. Instead of abandoning his dream of sharing the gospel as a preacher, Vincent instead found a new and—for him, at least—more effective way of doing so. His inability to excel at one form of evangelism may in fact have helped him to find another—his true "voice," which was painting.

From an early age, Vincent loved art, and when at age eighteen he went to work for his uncle, he initially enjoyed success as an art dealer. Even at this point, he understood that art can play a profoundly revelatory role, writing to Theo, "Painters understand nature and love her and teach us to see her." Vincent regarded great art as "food for life."

But eventually Vincent lost his heart for dealing in art. He began to see the buying and selling of art as a betrayal, in which the "value" of a work of art is assessed strictly in terms of the price it brings. To pretend that paintings are mere commodities, no different in principle from any other object that can be bought and sold at market, struck Vincent as a fraud. Though he could craft a secure and well-paying career for himself as an art dealer, he could not abide the failure to recognize art as the "food" it really is. He could not bear to see art treated as a mere commodity, and he eventually lost his job.

Vincent then resolved to become a preacher: "It is my fervent prayer that the spirit of my father and grandfather may rest upon me, that I may become a Christian laborer. Or that I may be shown the way to devote my life more fully to the service of God." Vincent's timeless quest could be unfolding today.

Next he immerses himself in the Bible, translating portions of it into other languages. His goal is not only to know it, but "to know it by heart and to view life in the light of its words." He becomes a minister's assistant and preaches his first sermon. It is not a success. He has difficulty remaining focused. He knows he is cut out for something, but he begins to sense that whatever it is, it may not be preaching from the pulpit.

He concludes his first sermon by painting a picture in words, evoking the image of a "landscape at evening, in the distance a row of hills in blue evening mist, above the splendor of the sunset, gray clouds with linings of silver, gold, and purple." Though from the vantage point of those in attendance at the service, his sermon falls flat, Vincent finds the experience personally moving: "When I was standing in the pulpit I felt like someone who, emerging from a dark cave underground, comes back to the friendly daylight." Sharing with others a vision of an unseen reality seems to be his calling. Yet his ability to do so as a preacher is about to be sharply constrained.

Vincent next goes to Amsterdam to study to become a pastor, a life that does not come easily to him. He writes to Theo, "I find it difficult to work, but I must work, because my life depends on it; it is nothing less than a struggle for my existence." But the results are disappointing. He fails his seminary entrance exam. He embarks on another course of theological study, but he fails that, as well.

Part of the problem, it seems, is that Vincent finds the study of dead languages such as Greek and Latin irrelevant, and he sees no reason why someone seeking to preach the gospel should be made to study subjects such as mathematics and geography. Convinced that he will never be able to pass the course of seminary study, he turns his attention to missionary work.

He goes to a Belgian mining village, whose denizens labor in some of the most inhospitable and impoverished circumstances anywhere in Europe. Though not a licensed minister, he spends his days ministering to the sick. His calling, as he sees it, is "to preach the gospel to the poor."

In fact, Vincent not only preaches to the poor but chooses to live like the poor. His abode is a humble shack, his bed is made of straw, and he dresses, eats, and lives like those to whom he preaches. Moved by the grinding poverty all around him, he eventually gives most of his possessions, including his clothing, to his neighbors. But he does not feel sorry for himself. In fact, he feels more closely connected to reality than ever before. He writes to Theo, "This life of suffering makes you love naked, living reality."

But even this most humble of dreams comes to an end. Before long Vincent is visited by an ecclesiastical inspector, who finds his profound zeal and manner of life bordering on the scandalous. The inspector reports back to his superiors, and Vincent soon is dismissed because of the squalid conditions in which he lives— conditions that threaten to "undermine the dignity of the priesthood."

Looking back on the experience, Vincent writes: "Nobody understood me. They thought me a madman because I wanted to be a real Christian. They turned me out like a dog, saying that I was causing a scandal because I tried to relieve misery."

To be denied the opportunity to pursue your calling is a terrible thing. Vincent truly believes—perhaps even knows as surely as he knows anything—that he has been called to help the poor by preaching the gospel. Yet the authorities keep telling him that he is unfit, that he doesn't have what it takes, and that he will never make it as a pastor.

Shaken to the foundations of his being, Vincent experiences a period of profound doubt. To Theo he writes: "How can I be useful? Of what service can I be? There is something inside of me, but what can it be?" He feels called to go on with his evangelism, but he has no money and no backing from the church. What can he possibly do? Can he turn his back on his vocation?

Then he realizes that he can carry on his evangelical work through images.

Vincent's Belgian mining community was a place without pictures. In fact, Vincent writes, "people here do not even know what a picture is." From a state of deep despair, he begins to "feel my energy revive, and I said to myself, 'I shall rise again. I will take up my pencil, which I had forsaken, and go on with my drawing.' From that moment, I was transformed."

He will continue his evangelism, but he will do so using not the spoken or written word, but the drawn and painted image. He will appeal not to the ear, but to the eye, reaching the heart by means of images.

Vincent's art will be different, radically different, at least from most of the art he had encountered in the professional art world. His images will capture not exalted and majestic subjects, but the humble, poverty-stricken miners he had been living with, types who, from his point of view, "had still not been portrayed in painting."

Vincent will be an artist, but an artist of a particular kind: one who uses his work to make visible what cannot be seen without painting. He will reveal the humanity of people others often regard as somehow subhuman. He will show the world what art really is—a reality pulsing with the divine presence. He will, in fact, become something new and urgently necessary—an evangelist in images.

Vincent sees the divine imprint in places artists had not looked for it before. "I prefer painting people's eyes to cathedrals," he writes, "for there is something in the eyes that is not in the cathedral; a human soul, be it that of a poor beggar or a streetwalker, is more interesting to me."

If this line of interpretation is correct, Vincent does not turn his back on religion, but rather finds a new way of leading a faithful life and spreading his faith. Art provides him with a new and far more fitting means of religious expression. He calls himself a "peasant painter," a calling he describes in these terms: "The work of the peasant painter has a white ray of light in comparison to which the sermon is black." He can light up things from the easel that he could never hope to illuminate from the pulpit.

Vincent says that believing in God does not mean obeying the sermons of prudes, but "knowing that there is a god, not dead or stuffed, but alive and urging us to love with an irresistible force." To capture this force in images, he will not engage in the iconography of religious history paintings, but instead capture the infinite in the subjects of everyday life—in sunflowers and irises, in wheat fields and light reflecting on water.

He admits that the written and spoken word have their places, but one can write in a picture as well as in a book, and "the real significance of what the great artists tell us in their masterpieces" leads just as surely to God. Vincent recognizes in himself a deep need for faith, but he responds to it in an unorthodox way, "by going out at night to paint the stars."

Vincent sees himself as performing a fundamentally Christlike service. He calls Jesus "the supreme artist," but one who "disdains marble and clay and color and instead works in living flesh." To come to this realization, however, Vincent must bump repeatedly against some very real constraints—namely, ecclesiastical conventions surrounding the proper nature of ministry and his own limitations as an orator. While these disappointments take a great toll on him, driving him on multiple occasions to a state of despair, they also lay the groundwork for per-ceiving and answering a very different form of calling—painting—the pursuit of which ultimately leaves the world deeply enriched.

In retrospect, Vincent's inability to pursue what he took to be his first calling was difficult to bear, but it would have been far worse had he succeeded as a pastor. To realize his full capacity to serve by sharing his vision of a world shimmering with the divine presence, he first had to suffer, and suffer terribly. His unusually strong sense of calling became for him a heavy burden, weighing him down with the feeling that he was wasting his life.

But his succession of failures helped him to more deeply understand the peo-ple he eventually aspired to serve—the poor and downtrodden who had so rarely been truly depicted in art, as well as Jesus Christ, whose very mission had been rooted in suffering.

Vincent's failure to become a preacher was not a meaningless interlude on the path to greatness. Instead, it served as the wellspring of his inspiration. It tor-mented and tested him, ultimately molding his vision to the point that he could depict things that no one else had managed to capture. He could at last serve the higher purpose for which he so urgently yearned. His failure was also his victory.

AFTERWORD

The Life of Service

WE COME TO LIFE WITH THOSE WE SERVE. THE WORDS ARE EASY TO SAY, BUT the lessons are not always so easy to bring to life. Our culture is brimming with the opposite message: We come to life by looking out for ourselves. We are told that devoting our time and energy to service necessarily diminishes us and saps us of life, leads to "burn out."

Yet consider the case of Victor Frankenstein, a man who, because he saw nothing greater than himself, sought to transform himself into the lord of a new creation. Instead of creating something new, however, his loveless monomania spawned only destruction, including his own. Or think of Ivan Ilych, whose ambitions were far more banal. He, too, led a life curved in on itself, robbing himself of the opportunity even to connect with—let alone to serve—another human being. By serving nothing and no one beyond themselves, both Victor Frankenstein and Ivan Ilych spent much of their lives dying rather than living.

Albert Schweitzer, on the other hand, devoted his life to service. He longed to be in Africa because he regarded it as his calling, the place where, perhaps more than any other, he came to life. Rebecca also had a place—a place in her family, and in history. She was wife and mother, prodding and cajoling the males in her life to become the men they were supposed to be. But she was also leading a world-historical life that rose to the level of myth, seeking to secure a blessing on behalf of all humankind.

Benjamin Franklin devoted his life to what Francis Bacon called the "relief of man's estate"—advancing knowledge, enhancing civic life, and instilling the habits necessary for people to govern themselves and each other justly. In constantly asking how he could serve his community, Franklin grew into a fuller and more fulfilled human being. Alexander Solzhenitsyn's story reveals possibilities of service that arise even in sickness and solitude—whether the affliction of a single individual or an entire society. Foremost among the forms this service took was simply to see and to speak the truth.

The stories of John Wooden and Bill Cook are considerably homelier, perhaps even to the point of being homespun. But the point in telling them is simply this: Opportunities to come to life through service are always ready to hand. Familiar activities such as teaching Sunday school, leading a group of scouts, coaching a sports team, or running a business can change someone's life. Cook was in many respects a seemingly ordinary person, but he operated with an extraordinary depth of belief in something—that trying something new can make an important difference in the lives of others.

Ebenezer Scrooge reminds us that redemption is possible. By seeing the stories of our lives writ large, new possibilities for service can open up and bring us to new life. Vincent Van Gogh is a real-life example of such a transformation. His aspirations to make a difference seemed blocked at every turn, but eventually he found a way through which he could share his deep conviction that the divine shimmers in the ordinary.

In reflecting on these stories—so different from one another in so many respects—I cannot escape the sense that two paths are always open to us. One is the path that leads inward, toward increasing self-preoccupation and the pursuit of wealth, power, and fame. The other is the path that reaches outward, seeking connection and contribution through service.

Ultimately, it seems to me, the crucial question is this: Can we make such a connection, one that puts our own preoccupations aside long enough simply to see and know another human being? Perhaps connection—both the source and the highest expression of service—is what life is all about. Consider one last story, this one drawn from my own experiences as a medical educator.

The second-year students were gathered in one of the medical school's amphitheater-style classrooms. A middle-aged father and his adolescent son entered through the door and went to the front of the room. The boy traveled by wheelchair, and it was apparent to everyone present that he was neurologically devastated. His posture was contorted, his head was tilted back and to one side, and his eyes stared blankly up toward the heavens, evidently registering nothing.

The father began to relate an account of a conversation he had had with his wife the evening before. She argued that they should not take their son to the medical school again. He had been poked and prodded by medical students for more than a decade, and the family had contributed far more than their share to the education of future physicians. It was time, she said, to let their son rest. He had been used as a pin cushion long enough.

Her husband disagreed. He maintained that it was important for each year's group of doctors-in-training to meet their son for themselves. The encounter would help them learn about his disease. More importantly, they would learn firsthand what it is like to be a parent and know that something is wrong with your baby, yet wait months for a diagnosis. These future physicians needed to feel what it is like to know that your beloved child has a relentlessly progressive and invariably lethal neurological disorder.

As the father told his story, his emotions often got the better of him. From time to time, he stretched out his hands to the students as though he were pleading with them, wanting them to understand how seriously he and his wife took the education of these doctors-to-be. As he spoke, particularly about their son's deterioration over recent years, he broke down on more than one occasion and had to collect himself. Students seated in the front rows could see his tears welling up in his eyes.

Throughout the father's story, one student seated in the fifth row was totally captivated, never averting his eyes from the speaker and his son. When the father winced, a grimace swept across the student's face. When the father sighed, you could see the student's shoulders fall ever so slightly. And when the father wept, the student's eyes welled up with tears. It seemed as though he was reliving the father's long struggle right along with him.

In the first row sat another student. This student reacted very differently to the father's story. No more than five minutes into the session, he reached down into his backpack, opened up his lecture notes, donned his ear phones, and spent the remainder of the hour tuned out. He evidently had concluded that the father's story did not contain any material that would appear on the upcoming exam. And since he cared about nothing more than his exam scores, he opted to devote his time to studying.

What are we to make of the conduct of these two students? Which one did a better job of learning during that hour? Which one was better prepared for the upcoming exam? Two years later, which one would the medical school faculty and administration point to with a greater sense of pride? Which of the two would their fellow students admire most? And perhaps most importantly of all, which of these two future physicians would each of us most likely turn to if a loved one needed care?

Such stories remind us that medical excellence is not strictly a matter of what we know. It is possible to be the most knowledgeable, technically skilled, widely published, extensively funded, and successful physician in the room but still leave a great deal to be desired as a doctor. Medical excellence is more than knowledge and skill. It is also a matter of who a person is. And who a person is shines forth in everything that person does. Patients want and need more from their doctors than mere expertise.

What else do patients need? They need physicians to be genuinely curious about them and to take a sincere interest in their lives. Arriving at a diagnosis and prescribing the appropriate therapy is important, but so is sharing in the patient's experiences.

Everyone gets sick; everyone dies—even doctors. Medicine may turn the tide for a time, but the end is always the same, and every human being needs someone with whom to share. Sometimes, patients need doctors to be human beings first and experts second.

Patients need someone who sees them as more than a malfunctioning machine that needs repair. Our sufferings can take many forms. What distinguishes human beings from other animals is the fact that our suffering is a problem for us. We not only feel it; we also try to make sense of it, to situate it in the larger context of our life stories, and to find in it some meaning and purpose—insights into where we have been, where we are, and where we have yet to go.

What makes a successful physician? Do numbers tell the tale?—the number of lines on a business card or the number of pages of a résumé? The number of square feet in a physician's house or the number of cars in the garage? The number of dollars in an investment portfolio? What do we tell medical students about what matters most to us, and what do we say by the manner in which we approach each patient encounter?

To excel as physicians and human beings, we must do more than diagnose and treat diseases. We must also care for others. This means offering compassion, courage, and hope. It means serving others before we serve ourselves.

Of equal importance is how effectively we cultivate this sense of mission in the minds and hearts of our successors. Will future physicians see excellence in medicine primarily as a matter of grades and test scores? When they muse on the worthiness of their practices, will they be calculating expenses and revenues? Will they set their hearts on conventional signs of success, such as prestige, authority, and income? Or will they think first of their patients, the human beings they have cared for, and the lives they have been privileged to touch and even become part of?

The two medical students in this story took very different paths. The student who never took his eyes off the father and son did well in school and today cares for patients in a thriving community practice. His income is not high, he holds no high offices, and he does not enjoy a particularly high profile in his community. Yet when I think about the kind of physician I would want to care for me or my family, his is one of the faces that first comes to mind. He is not only a fine doctor, but a real human being, someone who truly serves and cares for his patients.

And what of the other student, the one who used the class time to study? He did quite well on the exam. In fact, he kept doing well on all exams, and he eventually graduated at the top of his class. He is now in the midst of a high-powered medical career, making a name for himself and earning—by medical standards, at least—a very high income. Yet when it comes to finding a physician, I would not choose him. He knows a lot and can do a lot, but I suspect that he sees his patients, their diseases, and all the tests and therapies he uses in their care as somehow serving him. Perhaps to him, patients represent little more than opportunities to prove his own greatness.

The distinction between these two students and the physicians they have become is not merely moral. It is also vital. In my view, the first one is more alive than the second, precisely because he approaches his work as service to others. He is not using other people as a means to advance his own ends. Instead he genuinely connects with and serves others, and in this way, he comes more fully to life.

RICHARD B. GUNDERMAN is Chancellor's Professor of Radiology, Pediatrics, Medical Education, Philosophy, Liberal Arts, Philanthropy, and Medical Humanities and Health Studies at Indiana University. He is the author of *We Make a Life by What We Give*.

CPSIA information can be obtained
at www.ICGtesting.com
Printed in the USA
BVOW09s1435200917
495407BV00001B/91/P